PRAISE FOR *DISCOVE*

T0021420

"I love this book! Kodo Sawaki was one of the greatest and most influential Zen teachers of the twentieth century. He was a huge influence on my teacher Gudo Nishijima, as well as Shunryu Suzuki, author of *Zen Mind, Beginner's Mind*; Taisen Deshimaru, founder of AZI; and many others who became important in Zen Buddhist lineages in the United States and Europe. This book is a treasure. It's the first complete biography of Sawaki in English, as well as a compendium of some of his deepest and most profound teachings. Sawaki wasn't some airborne guru floating through the clouds. He began life as a tough street urchin, then faced some of the greatest tragedies of the twentieth century and emerged as one of the deepest and most relevant philosophers of our time. It's great to finally have this material in English. Arthur Braverman deserves tremendous praise for making it available to us. I will read it again and again." —BRAD WARNER, author of *Hardcore Zen*

"A fascinating portrait of an unforgettable Zen master. From unpromising beginnings in Japan's lower depths, Sawaki rose to become among the best-loved and respected Soto Zen teachers of modern times. Engrossing and illuminating . . . Sawaki's unmistakable and authentic voice can be savored in this fine translation, which will offer many Westerners their first glimpse of this compelling Zen personality."
—PETER HASKEL, author of *Bankei Zen*

"*Discovering the True Self* is the best new book in English about Kodo Sawaki Roshi's life and teachings and his influence on his disciples. Arthur Braverman is a skillful master of the English language, and he translates both the power and the sense of humor of Sawaki Roshi. Arthur Braverman is the best person to translate Sawaki's unique and colloquial Dharma expressions, because of his long practice and study. I would like to express my deepest respect and gratitude for his continuous efforts." —SHOHAKU OKUMURA,
translator of *Zen Teaching of Homeless Kodo*

"Philippe ReiRyu Coupey, in his new commentary on the Shinjinmei (*In the Belly of the Dragon*, 2020) states the importance of Kodo Sawaki and his disciples not just for the perpetuation but also for the reinvigoration of Zen in Japan and the West: 'Times change, circumstances change, languages change. Master Kodo Sawaki took the expression of the Way out of the antiquated context it had fallen into and brought it into modernity. Master Deshimaru and others of his generation [including Kosho Uchiyama and Gudo Nishijima] transplanted it into a Western context. And now it's up to us to make it understandable for today's generation.'

"Arthur Braverman does just this in his new work on Kodo Sawaki, *Discovering the True Self*.

"Traditionally, Zen masters have been immortalized in hagiographies and mythologies that have sometimes done as much disservice as service to the preservation and perpetuation of Zen. In his new book on the teachings of Kodo Sawaki, as in his other portraits in *Living and Dying in Zazen* and *The Grass Flute Zen Master*, Braverman gives us the undistorted humanity of his subject. We might say he 'mortalizes' the masters.

"The charismatic Kodo, with all of his contradictions, is displayed through a sharp if narrow lens: his devotion to zazen. As a result, the hyperactive, competitive, and scholarly Zen student becomes over time the tireless teacher of stillness (*shikantaza*), the advocate of no-gain Zen (*mushotoku*), and the professor for whom all of the Buddhist scriptures are but a footnote to zazen." —RICHARD REISHIN COLLINS, abbot

Kodo Sawaki in the garden at Sengakuji Temple
(Photograph courtesy of Daihorin Publishers)

DISCOVERING THE TRUE SELF

Discovering the True Self

Kodo Sawaki's Art of Zen Meditation

TRANSLATED, EDITED, AND
WITH AN INTRODUCTION
BY ARTHUR BRAVERMAN

COUNTERPOINT
Berkeley, California

Discovering the True Self

Library of Congress Cataloging-in-Publication Data
Names: Braverman, Arthur, translator, editor. | Sawaki, Kōdō, 1880–1965.
    Works. Selections. English.
Title: Discovering the true self : Kodo Sawaki's art of Zen meditation /
    translated and edited by Arthur Braverman.
Description: First paperback edition. | Berkeley, California : Counterpoint
    Press, 2020.
Identifiers: LCCN 2020000997 | ISBN 9781640093775 (trade paperback) |
    ISBN 9781640093782 (ebook)
Subjects: LCSH: Sawaki, Kōdō, 1880-1965—Teachings. | Spiritual life—Zen
    Buddhism.
Classification: LCC BQ9288 .D57 2020 | DDC 294.33/927092—dc23
LC record available at https://lccn.loc.gov/2020000997

Cover design by Alex Camlin
Book design by Jordan Koluch

COUNTERPOINT
2560 Ninth Street, Suite 318
Berkeley, CA 94710
www.counterpointpress.com

Printed in the United States of America

10 9 8 7 6 5 4 3 2

To the memory of Kojo Watanabe

All of Buddhism is a footnote to zazen.

—KODO SAWAKI

CONTENTS

PROLOGUE: TWO SAWAKIS

Kosho Uchiyama, the late abbot of Antaiji Temple, often quoted from the talks of his teacher Kodo Sawaki. Sawaki was renowned for translating obscure Buddhist terms into everyday language. It's not surprising that Uchiyama, after studying with Sawaki for over twenty-five years, would have acquired his teacher's talent for clarity and simplicity.

Uchiyama remarked on more than one occasion that Kodo Sawaki had charisma, and added that sometimes his charisma could become an obstacle to people understanding what Uchiyama referred to as the "Buddhist Sawaki." I believe what Uchiyama was referring to as the "Buddhist Sawaki" was the wisdom his teacher imparted that was not something based on a particular time and place—a teaching that transcended the culture and customs of Japan at the time.

So what was this charisma to which Uchiyama referred?

In 1973, I married the daughter of a Jodo Shin (True Pure Land) Buddhist priest. Jodo Shin Buddhism is a "faith only" sect of Buddhism where priests have had families since back in the days of its founder, Shinran, in the thirteenth century. After the shock of giving up his heir, my father-in-law decided to take me to hear a sermon of a famous Jodo Shin priest by the name of Kikuchi.* Reverend Kikuchi was ninety years old and still quite healthy. Since his daughter wasn't going to marry a Jodo Shin Buddhist priest, I guess my father-in-law thought he would at least indoctrinate me to their family religion. There were two priests giving sermons that night, Reverend Kikuchi and a Jodo priest whose name I don't remember.

The Jodo priest spoke first. His talk was not very stimulating. When it was Rev. Kikuchi's turn, from the beginning he created an atmosphere of friendly openness. He talked about why he was able to live so long (eat no more than 80 percent of what you would like to eat) and then told a few anecdotes having little to do with religion. Once his audience was relaxed, he added bits of Jodo Shin philosophy into his talk. He had everyone's attention.

Because Japanese is not my native language, I got tired of trying to follow every word, and my mind started to wander. I looked around at the faces of people glued to the priest's every word, their heads slightly bobbing in assent and some lips moving quietly. They were mostly older people, more women than men. As Kikuchi spoke, quoting the old masters, I could hear voices reciting *Namu Amida Buddha*—"I take refuge in Amida Buddha." The priest became more animated as he spoke, and the voices of the choir of *Namu Amida Buddha* rose accordingly. By the end of

* The oldest daughter in a Pure Land Buddhist family without sons is expected to marry a priest to take over their family temple.

the talk, it sounded like I imagined a revival meeting in the South would sound, with people losing their self-consciousness, inspired by voices from within.

Was this Kikuchi's charisma?

When we returned to my father-in-law's temple, I told my wife what I'd experienced. She explained that before all the new forms of entertainment—movies, TV, and theater—were available, temples were the places where people went for amusement. If there was no entertaining religious theater at that time, it would be left to the priest to make the evening enjoyable. That was where charisma became a plus for drawing crowds to the temples. This was particularly true of Jodo Shin temples, where Kodo Sawaki often went as a child.

PART I

~

The Life

Kodo Sawaki was raised in a town called Isshinden that had been formed around a major Jodo Shin temple, Senjuji. The town was divided into two zones, an inner and an outer. The inner zone was enclosed by a moat surrounding Senjuji, whose head priest ruled the town. The outer zone outside the moat, where Sawaki lived, was developed after the inner zone and comprised mostly shady businesses like gambling parlors and brothels. After Saikichi (Sawaki's given name) lost both parents, he was passed on to an uncle, who died soon after the boy moved in with him, and then was adopted by an associate of another uncle. His new adoptive father was a lantern maker who turned his house into a gambling parlor at night. His adoptive mother was a retired prostitute. They adopted the young Saikichi so that they could put him to work for them. If the boy did something wrong, his stepfather would beat him, and if he did not behave properly at home, his stepmother would hit him on the head with the bowl side of her lit pipe.

Saikichi was a tough street kid, and when he reached his teens, he no longer feared his stepfather. But he still felt like he was suffocating in this squalor created by his adoptive family and their friends, and he decided to run away. During his last year with his stepparents, he visited many temples in the neighborhood, all True Pure Land temples. He already had a gift for storytelling as a child, and if there were any charismatic priests in Ishinden when he was searching for answers to his dilemma at that time, they would have made a lasting impression on him. His experiences while living in Ishinden were a mixture of hard work, fighting to survive (which he seemed to have little difficulty with), and a growing interest in the religious life. He had once, as a child, seen a group of monks return to their temple after being out begging and reciting a Buddhist chant, and the peace he felt as he watched these monks contrasted with his present wretched condition. He never forgot it.

Saikichi ran away from his home in Ishinden, deciding to go to Eiheiji Monastery. It was a three-day trip. Though he arrived half-starved, he was elated. A monk at the gate tried to send him away, but he refused to leave. He said he would die rather than go back home. After sitting by the gate to the monastery for two days famished and disheveled, a monk in charge of the temple laborers took pity on him and allowed him to stay in the workers' quarters.

. . .

"From before I was old enough to remember," Sawaki said at one of his sermons, "my sister told me I was always getting into trouble. She said it was the biggest concern of my mother when she was on her deathbed. I was three years old at the time."* His mother felt his father was too easy on him and wouldn't be able to control him once she was gone.

Not much is known about Saikichi's birth father other than that he was a gentle man and, according to Saikichi's sister, her brother was always calm in his presence. This was a boy she described as the neighborhood terror. When his father died, he was placed in the guardianship of his aunt and uncle. Though his uncle treated him as an unwanted orphan who was nothing but another mouth to feed, Saikichi was still relatively happy to have a home. He would take his young spoiled cousin to a nearby temple where the neighborhood kids played. When the monks from the temple came back from their begging round, they would chant as they entered the temple. The young Saikichi was moved by the sense of calm he felt as the monks chanted in unison. It was a feeling he hadn't experienced since his time in the presence of his father.

Saikichi's time in Ishinden, where he was sent after the sudden death of his uncle, was a mixture of hopelessness in the presence of his adoptive parents and glimmers of a hopeful world when he visited a neighbor, Chiaki Morita, a young art student who invited Saikichi into his family's home. When Saikichi observed this neighbor's cultured home and the respect the family members showed each other, he realized not everyone lived a wretched life

---

* The quotes in this section, unless otherwise stated, are taken from Tokugen Sakai, *Sawaki Kodo Kikigaki* 澤木興道聞き書き [The Words of Sawaki Kodo] (Tokyo: Kōdansha Gakujutsu-bunko, 1984). The book tells the life of Kodo Sawaki in his own words from excerpts taken of his talks.

like his adoptive family and their friends. He knew then that he had to escape.

Sawaki tells this story in one of his sermons:

When I was nine years old, a man of about fifty died in the midst of sleeping with a prostitute young enough to be his granddaughter. It created quite a stir in the neighborhood. There were policemen, detectives, and a crowd of pedestrians gathered around the brothel. The grown-ups were taking turns peeking inside and gossiping about what they thought had happened. I was extremely quick then, so I used my power to maneuver between people's legs and made my way through the entrance and up to the second floor. We used to play hide and seek in the rooms up there, so I knew my way around and thought nothing of going in and out of the rooms on that floor.

That's when I saw the dead man lying on a futon and a young woman of about seventeen or eighteen years old, a prostitute, in her bathrobe, plopped down by the pillow looking unconcerned. Next to the corpse was a woman I assumed to be the dead man's wife, who probably had been called and who was wailing and holding on to him and grumbling.

"Oh … you … dying on me like this is one thing, but here of all places. It will cause a scandal."

Sawaki goes on to say that the incident gave him a feeling of emptiness that was stronger than anything he'd felt when his mother, father, or uncle died. "I also realized," he added, "that you can't really hide anything. Not only on the day her husband died, but for all the occasions after, from the funeral to the one-year, three-year, and seven-year memorials, people will be saying, 'He's the one who died on the second floor of that whorehouse in the midst of doing it.'"

. . .

Though Saikichi had a sense of right and wrong and realized that Ishinden was a place where there was much seediness, his relationship with the Moritas and his later trips to the Pure Land temples in the neighborhood showed him that there was also a world of beauty somewhere out there, and he hoped to be a part of that world. Despite those feelings, it would be a long time before the boy, who wouldn't hesitate to use his fists to settle disputes, would find a calm place either inside him or in the outside world.

At this point in the young Saikichi's life, he knew nothing of Zen Buddhism. If we think in terms of Zen's principle of inherent Buddha Nature, we can look at his development as a series of confirmations of a truth inherent already in his being. One came from a sermon at one of the Shin Buddhist temples when he made the round of temples in Ishinden. That sermon inspired him to go to Eiheiji with very little money or food. In Sawaki's words:

I clearly remember one sermon at a Pure Land temple [when I lived in Ishinden]. It was about Sessen Doji, who was willing to throw away his life to hear the second half of a poem pointing to the truth. When Sessen Doji lived in the Snow Mountains (the Himalayas), Tentaishaku (a god who protects the earth) took the form of Rasetsu (a flesh-eating demon) and appeared in front of Sessen and recited these two verses: "All things are impermanent / They appear and disappear." Upon hearing these words, Sessen was elated. "Let me hear the rest of the poem. If you do, I will be your disciple," he said. "I know the following verses," Rasetsu said, "but I am famished and can't say another word." Sessen couldn't bear not hearing the final verses and said, "If you recite the verses for me, I will let you eat my flesh." The demon then said, "Put an end to appearance and disappearance / Nirvana is realized." Sessen proceeded to carve the verses on trees, rocks, and roads and then climbed a tall tree and was about to jump to his death when Tentaishaku turned back into his original form and caught him. Sessen Doji was said to be Shakamuni Buddha in a previous life.

I didn't know the details of this talk at the time, but this young way seeker being willing to throw away his life to hear the true Dharma moved me greatly.

He thought he'd found the true Dharma when he arrived at Eiheiji Monastery and would be able to settle down there, but it turned out not to be that simple. After working for a while with the temple laborers, he was told by a monk that he would not be able to stay indefinitely.

"Eiheiji does not ordain," a monk he worked with told him. "You have to find a temple where you can be ordained, and then, with a request from that teacher, you can return to Eiheiji."

Sawaki talked about his feelings when he first arrived at Eiheiji, how he felt all the monks he saw were bodhisattvas. Then he met monks who promised him ordination if he went to their home temples. That was the beginning of his awareness that not every monk was a bodhisattva. One, in particular, was for him a real trickster.

One monk, who was caretaker at his teacher's temple—Choujuan in Maruoka, Echizen—said, "If you come to my temple I'll see to it you're ordained." I was elated. Anything to allow me to be ordained, I thought. I happily went to his teacher's temple. However, he turned out to be shrewd, in the worldly sense, but also a very lazy, degenerate monk. Under the guise of seeing that I would become a monk, his ulterior motive was to use me like a maid, working me to the bone. I wore old work clothes and worked myself ragged.

In the morning I'd fill up three buckets of water, read morning sutras, prepare rice gruel, and then do winter austerities.* This was in the middle of the coldest time of the year, and five in the morning. I did *takuhatsu* [begging] barefooted on the northern country snow-covered road. After exhausting myself in this way, I'd come back to find that lazy, good-for-nothing monk drinking sake with a woman. I realized that he sent me on *takuhatsu* so I wouldn't be around to see his misbehavior. Nevertheless, I continued devotedly to do the work without any complaints.

However, that silly monk took me for a weakling. He would constantly berate me. One day he was drinking with

* I assume this means winter begging.

a woman and picking at pieces of meat and yelling abuses at me. I grabbed him and dragged him from the parlor into the snow and beat him mercilessly. I pushed his face into the snow, and I walked away from the temple and returned to Eiheiji. When I think about that time in my life and how miserable I was, tears come to my eyes. At that time, however, I didn't feel regret at all.

Before Sawaki left Eiheiji Monastery to find a temple where he would finally be ordained, he was introduced to the practice of zazen by one of his fellow monks. He knew nothing of the practice before entering Eiheiji, knew nothing of Zen. He only knew, as a result of counsel from a Pure Land priest in Ishinden, that Pure Land priests were expected to marry and raise families. The priest told him that having a wife and children would make serious practice difficult, if not impossible. "I visited Eiheiji on my travels," the priest said, "and it was a place where genuine Buddhist practice prevailed. I would recommend you go to Eiheiji."

"If you're going to be a Zen monk," an Eiheiji friend told him, you have to learn how to practice zazen." The only thing the young Saikichi knew about zazen was a feeling like an electric shock going through him at the mere sight of the silhouette of four monks sitting in meditation on the other side of a screen when he went into the storage room to get some sugar for the temple cook. He walked quietly past the screen, feeling that what those monks were doing was a holy act. After the first lesson by the monk, he sat in zazen every chance he had.

On one occasion Saikichi went with a group of Eiheiji monks to assist at a ceremony at Ryuunji Temple. Ryuunji was a temple connected to Eiheiji. Saikichi was seventeen years old and still only a worker and not ordained. When the ceremony was over, the monks had some free time, so they went out to have fun. Saikichi, having become very serious about understanding zazen to its depth, remained behind and sat in zazen facing one of the sliding screens in one of the tatami-matted floors in a temple reception room. A woman who volunteered to help at the temple and had a tendency to boss Saikichi around happened to walk in on him while he was practicing zazen. Sawaki tells this story many years later on an NHK broadcast called *Religion Time*:

> I was practicing zazen when this maid who came to help with the food preparation was cleaning the bowls, reciting, "Praise the Buddha, praise the Dharma." She opened the sliding screen door to put the bowls away, and saw me practicing zazen. With a gasp, she bowed to me in prayer pose.
>
> At that time, I hadn't studied anything about Buddhism and knew nothing about [the philosophy of] zazen. This was a woman who ordered me around, and now bowed to me as if I were a Buddha—without a doubt there must be something [to this practice]. I felt then that zazen was something I should do all my life. I was seventeen and it was the end of the Obon festival.

At some time during his stay at Eiheiji, someone called Saikichi "Tetsugen," and the name stuck. The last few months at Eiheiji, he'd been called Tetsugen—the name having the ring of a monk.

. . .

Tetsugen was on the road, destination Soshinji Temple in Amakusa, Kyushu. A student of Koho Sawada Roshi who was training at Eiheiji had befriended Sawaki and convinced him to go to Soshinji, where he was sure his teacher would ordain him. Sawaki had no money, but his robe, though tattered, and his shaved head allowed him to stay the night at temples willing to accommodate him, and many would send him off the next morning with a box lunch. The hike from Eiheiji was arduous, but Sawaki was strong and determined. The hike across the country was the least of his problems. Not everyone he met believed he was a student of Buddhism. His ragged condition made some suspect he was a criminal disguised as a monk.

When he came to the Kuzuryu River, he would have to take a ferry across. Without a penny to his name, he joined the crowd and boarded the boat. When they reached the other shore, the captain came around to collect the fee. Tetsugen had to think quickly. He started reciting the Heart Sutra, stretching the recitation as long as he could, keeping his head down so he wouldn't make contact with the captain.

"When the ferry emptied out and it was only myself and the crew," Sawaki said, "I finally looked up at the captain and told him of my plight. 'I recited this sutra to help all sentient beings to enter the Buddha Land, and the fact is I have no money.' I was panicking inside. 'Please accept this recitation in lieu of the fee.'

"The captain looked down at me and laughed and allowed me to go."

Sawaki took this as a good omen and continued on his way with a new bounce in his step. Reading sutras out loud and doing *takuhatsu* on the road, he gave the appearance of someone full of confidence. In his own words, however, "I was not cheerful inside. My pocket was empty and the cold was severe." Crossing mountains in the snow with bare feet, he contracted frostbite. He realized he could never make it all the way to Kyushu like that, so he went to his older sister Sai's place. Sai and her husband had a fish store in Iga Ueno, a town famous as the home of ninja warriors and the birthplace of the poet Basho. When his sister saw him, he was so dirty she thought he was a beggar. When she realized it was her long-lost brother, they hugged. She screamed and pushed him away. He was full of lice. She made him take off all of his clothes and put them in a bucket of boiling water.

Until then Sawaki hadn't realized he was so full of lice. He reflected on how troublesome it must have been for all the temples he stopped at during his trek from Eiheiji.

At that time I was smothered in lice. From the time I left Eiheiji until I reached my sister's place, I had stayed in many temples on the way. I guess there was a big commotion at all those temples after I left. One I remember in particular was a Pure Land temple that took me in for the night and fed me. They asked me if I could repaper their *shoji* sliding doors. Having worked fixing paper lanterns at Ishinden, it was an easy job for me. The priest of the temple was impressed with my work and asked me to stay on for a few days giving me special treatment. And what did I leave him in return? A temple full of lice.

Sawaki stayed with his sister and brother-in-law until his frostbite healed, reminiscing with his sister about their lives as children. She took him around and showed him the sites of Iga Ueno. His brother-in-law tried to convince him to stay on permanently and work for them, but Sawaki was determined to become an ordained monk. He even refused to eat the fish they offered him.

Once back on the road, moving down from the mountains, the warmth made traveling easier. But it wasn't long before disaster hit again. Sawaki boarded a ferry from Otsu to Kobe. One of the passengers, a woman of about twenty-two or twenty-three years old who sat right in front of Sawaki, couldn't find her purse and created a big commotion about it.

In Sawaki's words, "Of all the passengers on board, I had the dirtiest outfit and was immediately suspect. 'I would never do anything like stealing,' I said. 'I came from Eiheiji Monastery and am on my way to Amakusa to continue my religious practice. It's true that I am poor, but I wouldn't steal even if my life depended on it.'"

When he got off the boat, a few policemen were waiting for him. They took him to the Kobe Minakami Prison, disregarding his pleas of innocence, and threw him in a cell and locked him in.

"No matter what I said in my defense," Sawaki said, looking back on this experience years later, "they were convinced that I was a thief and that was that." He only spent a month in prison and was eventually released at the request of a prison chaplain who believed his story. He was still a teenager at the time and felt that the world was coming to an end, but on reflection he said that the experience came in handy when, as a mature Buddhist priest, he gave talks to prisoners. "They trusted me because I could tell them of my own experience of being incarcerated."

Sawaki talked about his prison experience as being positive for the knowledge he received from it, but that wasn't what he felt when it was happening to him. "No matter how much I cried and cursed my fate," he said, "it did no good." His description of his period of incarceration was not without humor. He described how the apparent leader of a group of tough prisoners approached him and asked what he was in for.

"Hey, little monk, what'd you do to get yourself in here?" the boss man with his frightening frown asked. I was slouched over in the corner feeling very small. "Actually, someone on the same ferry as me misplaced some money and I was blamed for it. So I was thrown in here."

"So how much did you get?"

"Oh no, I didn't steal anything, but still I was treated like this," I said, as if I were pleading my case in court.

"You stupid bastard!" the boss man said, "We are murderers, arsonists, rapists, robbers, and there are many who haven't been caught still running loose, and you're in this place saying you didn't steal anything. What are you, an idiot?"

Sawaki went on to talk about how the prisoners made lives for themselves behind bars:

They would take a clump of rice and squeeze it until it was hard and solid and then carve it into a cube. Then they would take a piece of broken straw and poke indents in each of the six sides to create dice. Since there was nothing inside the prison that they could gamble with, they'd use the rice dice and bet with the only currency they had—their meals. They couldn't state their bets out loud because the guards would come and break up the game, so they quietly put up fingers indicating their bets. Some bet a meal, some two meals, and the cautious ones would bet a pickle. They were totally involved in the game. The big losers would go without food, some for a whole day. If they lost all their meals, they just sat quietly watching the game.

In reflecting on his short incarceration, he came to the conclusion that life inside the prison was not that much different than the lives of those men who lived in the outside world. "From the Buddhist point of view," he reflected, "we are all originally deluded beings," so he did not see a great difference between the prisoners and the prison guards.

After his release from prison thanks to the chaplain, his trip to Soshinji in Amakusa went relatively smoothly. He arrived at the temple in the spring of the thirtieth year of Meiji (1897) and was ordained by Koho Sawada Roshi the following eighth of December, the traditional date for the Buddha's enlightenment.

. . .

Sawaki's relationship with Sawada Roshi, the abbot of Soshinji, and with many of the people in the temple community was one of mutual respect. He was eighteen years old when he arrived, a rash young novice, energetic and willing to do whatever was needed in order to reach his goal of being ordained as a Zen Buddhist monk. The abbot paid careful attention to the goings-on at the temple and to the lives of his disciples. The new novice's energy did not go unnoticed. He took Sawaki under his wing, teaching him what the abbot was known for—reading sutras in a powerful and sonorous voice. Sawaki had a powerful voice, but a lot to learn before he could channel that voice into the proper pitch, rhythm, and tonal variation required to chant sutras. Sawada Roshi pushed his young disciple until he was satisfied that Sawaki had learned to make proper use of his sutra reciting voice.

Many years later when Sawaki described his time at Soshinji, he praised the abbot: "The priest Koho Sawada's calligraphy was highly skillful, his voice was outstanding, and his tone and melody when chanting sutras was first class. In addition, he composed poetry."

In Sawaki's first six months at Soshinji, along with learning how to project his voice to chant sutras, he learned how to perform Buddhist ceremonies. He was not only given special treatment by the master, but he became very popular among the parishioners. According to Sawaki, many parishioners made specific requests to Sawada Roshi to allow him to come to their houses to chant sutras at their altars for the memorials of their departed. All this favoritism did not go over well with the other monks.

Koun Yamamoto, the young monk who befriended Sawaki at Eiheiji, had recommended to Sawaki that he go to Soshinji to finally get ordained. He told Sawaki that his teacher Sawada Roshi was an authentic Zen master and that Sawaki wouldn't be disappointed when he studied under Sawada. He was convincing enough to get his young friend to travel halfway across the country to study at Soshinji. After a year training at Eiheiji, Yamamoto returned to Soshinji. Sawaki was excited to tell Yamamoto that he had indeed been ordained and that Sawada Roshi was everything Yamamoto had said about him. To Sawaki's surprise, however, Yamamoto was very cold to him. He started to boss Sawaki around and cursed him when he made mistakes, even striking him at times. Sawaki passively took it all, hoping that his older brother disciple would change once he settled back in Soshinji. In Sawaki's words, "Since I didn't strike back at Koun, he must have thought he could easily take advantage of me."

Not knowing Sawaki's past, Yamamoto had no idea how explosive his Dharma brother could be. Yamamoto's change in attitude toward Sawaki was at least partly due to the younger disciple's popularity with their teacher. Sawaki was to learn jealousy was not something that only existed outside of Buddhist temples. Sawaki being the newcomer, Yamamoto probably figured he could do whatever he wanted to his younger brother disciple and Sawaki would have to take it. That was, after all, the protocol at Zen monasteries. He was to learn that it wasn't always so.

The major confrontation came during the *segaki* ceremony.* Sawaki described it as follows:

* A ceremony of making oblation to the hungry spirits. It is held for the repose of the souls of the dead.

The villagers came to help in the kitchen with the food preparation. I dropped something and Koun hit me with the fire
shovel. That was the last straw. "What the hell do you think
you're doing?" I screamed. I grabbed his feet and threw him
down and beat him severely. Then I took his *fundoshi* [loin-
cloth], tied him up with it, and dumped him in a mud puddle.
Everyone stopped what they were doing, but nobody tried to
stop me. They knew Koun had been picking on me and were
pretty disgusted with his behavior. They seemed ready to back
me up. [I heard someone say,] "I thought Kodo was just a nice
guy, but he finally fought back," and many applauded me.
Sawada Roshi entered the kitchen and supported me, saying,
"Kodo bore it as much as he could, and finally let it all out."

Koun Yamamoto fell out of favor, even with the teacher. He
soon left Soshinji.

. . .

Much of what Sawaki experienced in his two years at Soshinji
helped inform his later life as a monk and Zen teacher.

When Sawaki was nineteen years old, he was asked to read a
sutra for the death of the father of a man named Tou, whose family was the poorest in an impoverished village. Sawaki described
Tou as a "little slow mentally." The house, more like a shack, was
dilapidated—four posts, no tatami, with chaff laid directly on an
earthen floor. Tou's father was laid on two straw mats. "When I
arrived at Tou's house," Sawaki said, "I looked around and saw

only the corpse. I wondered where Tou was. Then I noticed him lying down quietly in the corner opposite his father. He was completely naked, not even a loincloth. 'Hey, Tou,' I said, raising my voice. 'What the heck are you doing there? Your father died and here I am.'"

Tou told Sawaki that he and his father had only one kimono between them, so he put the kimono on his father inside out, and he had nothing to wear.* Even the kimono the dead man wore was old and ragged. Sawaki immediately took off his robe and his own dilapidated kimono, and the two of them stood there stark naked (Sawaki too had no loincloth). He told Tou to put on his kimono and gave him his own sash to tie it with. In Sawaki's words, "At that time I too was poor and there really wasn't much difference between Tou and me. Neither of us had a loincloth. I put on my monk's robe over my naked body and returned to Soshinji." Sawaki stole three *sho* of rice, took the little savings he had and returned to Tou's shack.† "Take this money," he told Tou, "and buy some tofu, then come back here, cook the rice and invite your neighbors to take part in a wake. I'll come back tomorrow and conduct the funeral."

In future lectures Sawaki often condemned those monks who perform funerals in order to get contributions. He said, "They make me sick to my stomach."

. . .

* Perhaps it was a custom to dress a corpse with the kimono inside out.
† One *sho* is approximately 1.8 liters or 0.48 gallons.

As Sawaki explained, in the Zen sect a monk finds a temple where he can train, follows the teaching of the master, becomes ordained, and once he has learned all the basics, heads out into the world as an *unsui*, staying at training temples searching for a teacher with whom he can deepen his practice.* He complained about the present condition of monks whose interest is in finding a temple where they can be priests and settle down as heads of temples. "These fellows are not really true monks," he said.

After more than two years training at Soshinji, Kodo Sawaki, following the traditional way of an *unsui*, put on his umbrella hat, his sandals, and robes, and set out to seek a teacher for whom he felt an affinity, to further his Zen practice. He was most likely unaware that all kinds of political and military intrigue were going on at the time because Russia and Japan were both interested in controlling parts of a weak Imperial China.

In a lecture on the *Shodoka* (Song of Enlightenment) many years later, Sawaki commented on the part of the text that reads "I have wandered along rivers and oceans, crossed mountains and waded streams. I searched for a master to ask about the Way and practiced Zen meditation." He talks about how at the time (1962), students took professors' courses even if they disliked the teacher and were only concerned with passing tests. If the teaching was not going to be on a test, they didn't care about it. However, in the old days, monks traveled around searching for a teacher. They would spend a night at a temple, have breakfast the next morning,

---

* An *unsui* is a "floating cloud" or novice monk who travels from monastery to monastery.

and meet with the head priest. If they weren't impressed with the teacher, they would move on. If they liked what they felt from the teacher, they would stay and study with him. That was *unsui angya*, the name for *henzan* (a term meaning "visiting masters," a title of one of the chapters of Dogen's *Shobogenzo*).

. . .

Sawaki settled on a temple in Tamba called Entsuji. The teacher's name was Senmyo Hara. Most of the twenty or so monks were from the Tamba area, and Sawaki, like one or two others not from that region, was looked upon as an outsider. At twenty years old, and still a rash youngster, Sawaki didn't take kindly to being looked down upon by other monks, and he made it clear that he wasn't going to be humiliated by anybody. He also had an insatiable appetite—he never seemed to get enough to eat. When Hara Roshi took him with a group of monks to perform a ceremony at another temple, at mealtime Sawaki gobbled up the food before anyone else was halfway through and jumped up to get a second helping, and a third. The roshi reprimanded him for eating so fast and so much. But in Sawaki's words, "It was a very mild reprimand," and he told his teacher he didn't know how to eat slower than that. Sawaki also said that the monks at Entsuji were very complacent, and he tried to stir them up in various ways. Besides these mild reprimands, Hara didn't seem to know how to handle him.

Sawaki's insatiable appetite was probably due to his limitless energy. When he arrived at Soshinji, he was called Tetsugen, the nickname given him at Eiheiji. The first character, *tetsu*, means "iron." After the Soshinji community got to see his movements, they began to call him Tetsubin, which means "iron pot." They called him Iron Pot because, they said, he was always bubbling with energy. Until Sawaki learned to control his abundant energy, it revealed itself in ways that made community life difficult. He didn't like lazy or passive monks and he didn't hide those feelings. He also practiced zazen when the others slept or took breaks from their daily chores, which didn't endear him to his Dharma brothers.

One incident that Sawaki's biographer Tadao Tanaka writes of was when young Kodo lifted his robe and one leg and let out an enormous fart. This was in response to an intellectual discussion some Entsuji monks were having, a discussion Sawaki felt had nothing to do with the real essence of Buddhism. He listened until it became too much for him, then farted and walked out of the room. He was known for those kinds of antics because he liked to be a gadfly to those he deemed too full of themselves. Hara Roshi was mild mannered, and his soft approach to dealing with his disciples had been sufficient up until he had to confront Sawaki. He didn't know how to handle his new young student; the master's gentle reprimands didn't seem to have much effect.

When Hara asked Sawaki and another monk to help out at Ryuunji at the request of Ryoun Fueoka Roshi, he was secretly happy. He'd had enough of what he considered weak-kneed monks, and though he liked Hara, he knew this easygoing priest was not the kind of teacher he needed. Fueoka knew the trouble Sawaki was to his Dharma brother Hara, but Fueoka enjoyed the challenge of working with the rambunctious Sawaki. It may even have reminded him of his own master, the famed Nishiari Zenji. When Fueoka requested Sawaki come to help out at his home temple in Kyoto Prefecture, Hosenji, both Hara and Sawaki were more than okay with the arrangement.

Sawaki tells of the first time he met Fueoka Roshi, which probably forecasted to the master what he would be up against training this young rascal.

My first encounter with the priest Ryoun Fueoka happened when I was assigned to carry the box lunches for a group of priests including Fueoka and Hara who were to participate in an ordination ceremony at Ryuunji. The priests walked from Entsuji, leisurely talking and enjoying the walk. I wasn't interested in small talk, so I walked ahead of them, unaware of how far ahead of the group I had traveled. At lunchtime I looked around me and nobody was in sight. At that time I had been a couple of miles ahead of them. I sat and waited. By the time the others showed up, it was hours past lunchtime and they were all famished. Fueoka never tired of ribbing me about how hungry they all were that day.

. . .

Ryoun Fueoka was the first priest to have a lasting effect on Sawaki. "The strongest influences on me," Sawaki was later to say, "were my neighbor and childhood friend in Ishinden, the art student Chiaki Morita, the priest Ryoun Fueoka who I served as an attendant in my youth, and the students in the Fifth High School who I worked with at Daijiji Monastery in Kumamoto Prefecture in my later years."

Sawaki stayed with Fueoka at his home temple, Hosenji in Kyoto Prefecture, until a surprising turn of events took him from the one teacher for whom he felt a true affinity. Fueoka was a very unassuming priest, who, in Sawaki's eyes, was the embodiment of Dogen's teaching. He served as attendant to the famed and dynamic Dogen scholar, Nishiari Zenji. Though these two teachers couldn't have appeared more different from each other, they felt a real close connection. Fueoka was physically frail and had a soft, quiet persona, but he conveyed a firm confidence in his bearing that served as a stronger presence than teachers of far greater dynamic behavior.

A famous story of an incident when Nishiari was in charge of a monastery called Kasuisai shows how Fueoka could deal with the volatile Nishiari, and perhaps why he showed such an interest in the young Sawaki. Nishiari was overseeing a group of monks during a morning service when the monk hitting the *mokugyo* missed a beat and everyone was thrown off in the chanting.* Nishiari became livid. He lined everyone up and began to scold the whole group. But once he started yelling, he didn't seem to know how to stop. The rant went on and on as all the monks sat there in formal kneeling position with their eyes to the ground. One monk managed to sneak away and ran to Fueoka's room, where he was working on the ledgers for the temple.

---

* A *mokugyo* is a fish-shaped wooden drum used to keep rhythm during chanting.

"Osho, please do something," the monk pleaded.* "Roshi is screaming at us for making a mistake in the chanting, and it has been going on for over two hours now."

Fueoka quietly looked up from his ledger, closed it, put down his pen, and stood up. The monk followed him as he walked across the hall and into the zendo. Nishiari was still screaming at the monks and walking back and forth.

Fueoka looked directly at his teacher and Nishiari looked back at him. The master's tirade ceased as he was thrown off his pace. Then Fueoka went over to the monk in charge of the drum, took the stick, and said, "Okay, let's start again." The chanting resumed, and nothing more was said of the incident.

Though Sawaki was officially registered at Entsuji under Hara's supervision, he ended up spending most of his two years with Fueoka at the master's home temple, Hosenji. At some time during Sawaki's term under Fueoka's guidance, he massaged his teacher's neck. Fueoka felt so good after the treatment, he asked Sawaki to come again and again, and the massage sessions became a regular occurrence. While the young Sawaki was learning from the lectures and the meditation practice at Hosenji, it was during the private talks while he massaged his frail teacher's body that he really learned Fueoka's most important teaching. The seeds of what were to become Sawaki's constant refrain in his mature years—*mushotoku* (no-gain) Zen—were planted in his heart at this time. He remembered when his friend Chiaki Morita from Ishinden told him of the famous art teacher Ikkei Ukita,

---

* Osho is a term commonly used for the head priest of a temple.

who lived in a hovel in Kyoto and took a bare minimum fee for his paintings. It presented the thirteen-year-old Sawaki with the idea of doing something for its own sake and not so he might gain something from it.

Sawaki was twenty when he arrived at Entsuji. After a few months he went to Hosenji at Fueoka's request and remained with the master until he, Kodo, was drafted into the army just before his twenty-second birthday. Though some of those important lessons he'd learned from Fueoka were temporarily buried inside him during his war years, they were teachings that were to define him for the rest of his life.

Sawaki had been extremely competitive throughout his life as a youngster and he applied that competitiveness diligently to his Zen practice. "Those days," he said when telling of his massage sessions, "all I could think of was that I wanted to experience satori. I did everything I could to make my desire to become enlightened possible. This did not go unnoticed by my teacher. During one of our evening massage sessions, Fueoka commented, 'Kodo-san, I notice you've been practicing zazen even when the others are resting or studying. What's the reason for such intensity?' When I said, 'I want to attain satori,' he responded, 'You're like someone with a piece of shit on his nose running around wondering who farted.'"

During another massage session, Fueoka told Sawaki that many young Zen monks read that Zen is outside the scriptures, and they think they don't need to study the general Buddhist teachings. "They are making a big mistake," the master said. "To really understand Dogen's teaching, you should have a background in the early Buddhist scriptures as well." While Fueoka lectured on many of Dogen's writings, it was the practical advice during these private sessions that really had a lasting effect on Sawaki.

. . .

Sawaki had finally found the kind of teacher he'd dreamed of, only to have his dream shattered when a notice came by way of Entsuji to report for a physical at his local draft board. When he went to Entsuji to pick up the notice, Hara Roshi handed him a package.

"Open it," his old teacher said.

Sawaki opened it and found a new loincloth in it. Hara knew that Sawaki didn't own a loincloth, and the master didn't want him to be laughed at, or scolded, for going to the physical exam without one. Sawaki knew that Fueoka was his true teacher, but realized then that the abbot of Entsuji was concerned about him, and even sending him to study with Fueoka was done for Kodo's sake and not to get rid of a troublesome student.

The draft notice came months later. He had passed his physical exam and had been chosen from the lottery. The year was Meiji 33 (1900), and he would be required to spend three years in the army. He was strong, agile, and learned quickly, so he had no trouble fitting in. But all the detailed rules he had to follow in a peacetime army drove him crazy. He couldn't wait to be through with his service so he could get back to his Buddhist studies. While he was counting the days until his release, a power struggle was going on between Japan, who was determined to stake a claim as premier power in Asia, and Russia, who was also taking advantage of China's weakness to get a foothold in the territories of Manchuria and the Chinese vassal state of Korea. The two countries were the dominant nations of northeast Asia.

Finally, Sawaki's three years came to an end and he was to receive his discharge papers. In Sawaki's words, "I was forced against my will to put off my Buddhist studies. I could do nothing about it. You could call it a catastrophe. Soon, however, I thought I would receive my discharge and this time I would really devote myself to my studies. Just then, the Russo-Japanese war was threatening; I was called up to serve again, after my original term was over. My earnest hope to practice the Way hit another obstacle. It was the first and last time I ever composed a poem:

My one dream
To dedicate my life to Buddha
But fate has me
A country-defending devil

Sawaki talked about all the rules they were required to follow during his three years prior to the breakout of war with Russia. He said that his Zen training prior to being drafted helped keep him from breaking rules and receiving citations. He compared wartime military service with his first three years in the army, surprisingly considering life during the war easier to deal with. He felt that the training designed to prepare the soldiers for war did nothing of the sort. "You were reprimanded by your drill leader if you saluted with your hand at a 40-degree angle from the horizontal instead of the 'proper' 45 degrees," he said, "and you were then sent to the division head, who would smack you across the face and send you to the troop commander, who would write out a citation, which would be kept on file." Though Sawaki avoided citations, as he watched others receive them, he would reflect on the stupidity of it all, and for that he had to postpone his dream of studying the Buddha Way.

Kodo Sawaki on the left in military uniform
(Photograph courtesy of Daihorin Publishers)

Once the war began, Sawaki had little time to brood over his postponed dream.

On February 8, 1904, the Japanese army attacked the Russians without warning at the naval base at Port Arthur. The Russo-Japanese War had begun.

Sawaki didn't know how he would respond when the actual fighting began. The thought of Russia, a country that dwarfed Japan, gave him images of giant Russian soldiers, but when the fighting started, he surprised himself at how the fear disappeared. He saw his commanding officers prone with their heads buried in the ground, and it reminded him of the cowardly gang members in a gang fight he and his adoptive father had accidently run into when delivering lanterns in Ishinden. Both gangs had been screaming insults back and forth while swinging sticks and swords with their eyes closed. Sawaki was thirteen years old at that time, and the fear he saw in his adoptive father made him lose respect for this man who used to beat him regularly. He never feared his father again. Here, too, he saw his drill sergeant, who used to act like a tough guy smacking all the inductees around, with his head buried in the ground. It was another rude awakening for Sawaki:

When I looked around not one of our men even lifted his head. Not only were they not attacking, nobody even said a word. If we continued this way, how could we have any effect? I stood up and looked in the direction of the enemy. I realized that though they were shooting their weapons, few bullets were actually coming in our direction. I ran over to the squadron com-

mander and screamed, "Did you give the order to fire, or not?"
"Don't fire yet," he said with his head still buried in the dirt. I
saw the sergeant major, who was always throwing his weight
around, boasting, and pressuring all of us under him [during
peacetime drills]. He remained mute, his face pale as a ghost as
he hid in his trench trembling.

I started nudging everyone with the butt of my gun. Not
only the squadron commander, I ran around screaming at everyone. Finally we started advancing.

This incident apparently got the soldiers wondering who this
crazy soldier was. When they realized he was a Zen monk, they
assumed that Zen monks were fearless.

. . .

On August 31, the Thirty-Third Infantry Division attacked the
First Siberian Army. Sawaki was shot through the neck, the bullet splitting his tongue and knocking out some of his teeth. When
he regained consciousness, he was in a field dressing station with a
white tag tied to him. The white-tagged wounded were the worst
off and were treated last, assuming they would die anyway. After
days lying there, conscious but unable to move or speak, someone
finally noticed he was breathing and called one of the medics to
treat him. The medics treated Sawaki as best they could, and then
put him on a train with other wounded to be taken to Japan.

When they arrived in Japan, the wounded were taken from
the boats on stretchers. Old women and little children lined the

paths saying prayers for the safe return of these wounded soldiers. Sawaki went in and out of consciousness. When he saw all those people along the side of the road with their hands in prayer pose, he wondered whether he had not already arrived at that other world.

Sawaki was soon transferred from Hiroshima to Nagoya, where he was treated for his wound and convalesced in the Nagoya hospital for two months. Though still officially in the army, he was allowed to go to his home at Ishinden for rest and recuperation.

It was over eight years since he'd run away from home. Whatever feeling of excitement he may have had at seeing his hometown again was short lived. He describes his arrival at his adoptive parents' home: "I opened the front door and was thrown into a state of shock. My adoptive mother Hisa's hair was a mess, her kimono was open, and she was surrounded by her own feces. A chain tied her to the chair. Still, this shit-stained woman recognized me. 'Whaa!' she screamed and grabbed for me. I rarely am startled, but this time I had a horrid sensation. My adoptive mother had truly gone insane."

Sawaki's adoptive father, Bunkichi, was nowhere in sight, so he left the house and went around the neighborhood asking where Bunkichi was. He was told that the old man was out gambling and hadn't returned to his home in three days. Then Sawaki went to the local pharmacy where they all used to go to hang out, and he ordered some lunch. Just then Bunkichi stormed into the pharmacy, his sleeves rolled up, and he started his tirade.

"Mom's gone crazy . . . our business is failing . . . and I don't know how we are going to eat from now on . . . up until now you've been a monk . . . you've had your fun doing as you please, but I can't let you continue in this way."

Unfair as his self-centered adoptive father sounded, Kodo tensed up. It wasn't exactly a welcome home speech allowing him to fully recover from his wound. He knew that in his present condition he couldn't earn money to help his family. Though Bunkichi may not have been as psychotic as his wife, he was just as difficult to reason with.

After Bunkichi ran out of the pharmacy and back to his game, Sawaki found out that his adoptive father was banking on his death. If his adopted son had been killed in the war, Bunkichi would have received compensation from the government for the loss of his son. Bunkichi had gambled and used the expected compensation as collateral, and now he was in deep trouble, owing money to gangsters. Sawaki went to his older brother in Tsu, whom he hadn't had contact with in years, and borrowed money from him. He gave the money to Bunkichi, but that wasn't the end of it. Every time he met his adoptive father, it was the same story—money, money, money.

It is not surprising that Sawaki had an aversion to money and marriage for the rest of his days. Despite the unreasonableness of his adoptive father's demands, he truly felt sorry for the man. Bunkichi had become a victim of the low life he created for himself.

While Sawaki was in the hospital recovering from his wound, he met a fellow soldier, Irie, who was the head priest of Teiganji Temple. While that priest was recovering from his wounds, he asked Sawaki to temporarily take charge of his temple. Sawaki gave Bunkichi whatever money he had and asked his adoptive father to use it to care for Hisa. Then he went to Teiganji and performed the duties of a head priest for ninety days while Rev. Irie remained in the hospital recovering from his wounds. During this time Sawaki attended lectures by Joshin Murase, a Pure Land priest who had studied at the Kangakuin school of Buddhist studies at Horyuji Monastery in Nara. Murase was lecturing on the Buddhist teaching of the Consciousness Only school. Sawaki attended every lecture, asking Murase detailed questions about this ancient school of Buddhism.

Simply put, the Consciousness Only or *Yogacara* school of Buddhism is a teaching that declares that things exist only as processes of knowing and not as individual objects. The so-called external world is purely mind. Just as there are no actual objects experienced in the external world, there is no subject who experiences.

You can find evidence of Shinran's Pure Land Buddhism throughout Sawaki's talks on Zen, and also traces of the Consciousness Only school. These influences are what I believe make Sawaki's talks on Zen so unique. His understanding of the Consciousness Only school allowed him to explain ideas such as original enlightenment and its seemingly contradictory idea of the need for Buddhist practice that was so important to understanding Dogen's Zen. It also made the intellectually minded students, many who were in his audience, feel that Sawaki had a truly deep understanding of Buddhism as well as Zen.

Sawaki's connection to Pure Land Buddhism and its belief that we are all deluded—saved by Amida's vow and by zazen in

Sawaki's approach—connected him to the average believer, many of whom were country folk from farming families and might not have been interested in understanding philosophical explanations of Buddhist theory.

. . .

Sawaki was officially discharged from military service in January 1906. He was twenty-seven years old. That summer he returned to Soshinji in Amakusa and received Dharma transmission from Koho Sawada's Dharma heir Zenko Sawada.

According to Sawaki, his teacher Koho Sawada wanted him to take over Soshinji when Sawada retired, but because he was younger than Sawada's longtime disciple, Zenko, his teacher couldn't do it. So he had Zenko give Sawaki transmission.*

Not having a background in Buddhist studies, Sawaki remembered his teacher Fueoka's warning: "Don't be like those Zen students who know nothing of Buddhist teachings other than the colorful Zen stories. They act out their own stories and think they are real Zen men. They don't realize that the wild Zen stories they read about were actually timely incidents created by teachers who knew what they were doing, teachers who were well versed in Buddhism." Fueoka realized that Kodo, having a wild streak, could easily fall into that trap if he didn't understand Buddhist

---

* Transmission in Soto Zen Buddhism is really a ceremony in which the teacher gives his student permission to teach the Dharma. It is not, as many Westerners believe, a certificate indicating that the student is enlightened.

teaching. He didn't want his special student to take those stories as a license to behave as he pleased.

The seeds of caution Sawaki received from Fueoka, the teacher he considered one of the most influential people in his life, really started to take hold at this time.

Sawaki had received a stipend from the government for valor in action and used the money to take care of his adoptive parents, mainly paying off Bunkichi's debts, while he lived as frugally as possible. He said that being poor and eating little and sleeping less didn't bother him. What really concerned him was how far behind in his studies he was at twenty-seven years old. Twenty-year-old monks knew a lot more about Buddhism than he did.

. . .

The next six years Sawaki studied in Buddhist schools outside of Zen. The first two years were spent at the Takada branch, a sect of Shin Buddhism, and the next four years were at Kangakuin at the Horyuji Monastery in Nara. One can only guess that it was Fueoka's caution that he study early Buddhism before jumping into Dogen's writing that encouraged him to learn from other Buddhist schools.

Sawaki had lived in Ishinden until his fifteenth year, where Shin Buddhism was the only school of Buddhism in town, and all the temples were connected with the Takada sect. If he were to grasp the real meaning of Shinran's teaching, however, it would have been during these two years at the Takada sect Shin Buddhist school.

Though there were many sects of Shin Buddhism, they were all based on the teaching of its founder, Shinran. For Shinran, Amida's vow saved him, despite the fact that he was a deluded person. One does not practice (or in the case of Shin Buddhism, recite the *nembutsu*) in order to be born in the Buddha Land, but rather recites the *nembutsu* out of appreciation that he or she is already saved. When one recites the *nembutsu* with his or her whole heart, that person is saved at that instant. In a letter to his followers, he quotes his teacher Honen as saying, "The person of the Pure Land tradition attains birth in the Buddha Land by becoming his foolish self."

Though Zen Buddhists are considered believers in self-power, and hence will not be born in the Amida's Pure Land according to Shin Buddhists, this shows a lack of real understanding of Kodo Sawaki's Zen. It's true that at the time Sawaki studied at the Takada branch of the Shin Buddhist school and at the Kangakuin in Horyuji, he was still chasing after enlightenment, studying day and night, eating little, and practicing zazen whenever he had time—but the idea of giving oneself up to zazen was slowly being planted in his psyche. Like Shinran, Sawaki considered himself a *bompu* (a deluded person) and more and more he treated zazen as a power that saved him, not unlike the Amida vow was to Shinran.

. . .

What we know of Kodo's studies at the Kangakuin at Horyuji, Nara, is primarily how diligently he studied; we know little about the content of his study. I don't see a great influence of the Yogacara teachings, or Consciousness Only as it was also referred to, in Sawaki's talks when he preached around the country in his mature years. He was, according to his biographer, Tadao Tanaka, given the rank of *iko*, the second highest rank in the Yogacara school. He said that he liked to study and had to work hard to catch up with the other students whose studies were not interrupted by the war. His understanding of this deeply philosophical school may have given depth to his understanding of some of Dogen's more philosophical chapters in his monumental *Shobogenzo*. But the main reason for Sawaki's popularity was his ability to explain zazen in a way that made it real for lay practitioners as well as monks. Also, his love of the practice came through so clearly when he talked about Zen meditation, it made those who never practiced it want to give it a try.

At Kangakuin, Sawaki was famous for living on the bare minimum—rice, soybeans, soy sauce, and pickles. In addition, he slept very little. Though he had a lot of energy, he said he looked like an old man—prematurely aged from lack of sleep and nourishment. All he cared about was his studies. Rev. Join Saeki was in charge of the school. Saeki was quite open with his notes, allowing all his students to copy his lectures. His open attitude toward his study notes was not the rule at the time. Sawaki respected Saeki's attitude and followed this teacher's approach in later years when he prepared study notes for his own students.

Sawaki was very competitive at this time and studied day and night. It wasn't until he read Dogen in detail that he realized what his first teacher, Fueoka, was trying to point out.

As he read Dogen he felt as if his eyes were opened.

At this time Sawaki had an experience that had a profound effect on the understanding of his own image as a fearless man. During his war experiences, he proved to his fellow soldiers that he was courageous in battle. Some attributed it to the fact that he was a Zen monk. But the more he studied the Zen of the master Dogen, the more self-reflective he became. He relates one incident in which he learned that after returning to regular peacetime life he was becoming what he referred to as weak-kneed:

"It was the fortieth year of Meiji [1907]; there was an explosion in the Sumiyoshi gunpowder warehouse. I was renting a room in a doctor's branch office in Nara. There was a thunderous rumbling and the doctor's flasks banged against each other. Before I realized it, I was shaking. Then I realized how I'd reacted. During the war my life was in danger many times but I was never afraid. I wondered why I was so startled this time."

He goes on to talk about how he realized that his lack of fear for his life during the war was nothing more than a result of his rivalry with others. He realized that he persevered because he was competing.

"I realized that I wasn't really settled to my *hara*. After learning the teaching of Dogen Zenji and practicing zazen I realized, 'Aha!' my actions during the Russo-Japanese war were nothing more than equivalent to the behavior of Chuuji Kunisada . . .* As a disciple of the Buddhist ancestors, I should be ashamed of myself."

When Sawaki read Dogen's *Gakudoyojinsho* (Points to Watch

* Kunisada was a gangster of the Edo period.

in Studying the Way), it confirmed his feeling that true practice is much more difficult than acting brave.

"'Breaking one's bones and crushing one's marrow to study the Way is thought to be difficult, but harmonizing the mind is even more difficult,' Dogen says, adding, 'However, harmonizing one's mind while controlling one's physical actions [i.e., following the precepts] to study the Way is most difficult.'"

Sawaki goes on to say that when you become excited because you are competing with others you can seem brave, but that doesn't compare with putting your mind in order as Dogen suggests. Now, he says, he bows his head in front of Zen Master Dogen.

. . .

Sawaki was moved to practice zazen before knowing much, if anything, about Dogen's teaching. When we choose a teacher, it is because there is something within us that resonates with that teacher. So it is not necessarily something new that we've come across, but rather something in us that we may not have known was there.

From the time Sawaki was the young Saikichi, his mind seems to have been in a state of confusion. He was adopted at a young age by unsavory people in a neighborhood where many of the neighbors were in illegal businesses, and he had to try to fit in. Because he was strong and tough, he did fit in. But in the back of his mind there was a desire for a better life. Though he knew nothing about meditation, Buddhism represented to him a better life. When Sawaki was nine or ten years old, he would take his young cousin to play in the yard at Tennoji Monastery—a Soto Zen monastery near his uncle's home. There he watched monks coming home from begging, chanting the Heart Sutra. The peace he felt as he listened to the monks chant exemplified the better life he'd sought.

. . .

After years of Pure Land and Consciousness Only studies, Sawaki was ready to return to Dogen. His studies in the Kangakuin of Consciousness Only or Yogacara had to help him better understand some of Dogen's more philosophical teachings, though it is Dogen's treatises on zazen that were most important to him.*

In the spring of 1912 Sawaki attended a *genzoe* at Eiheiji Monastery. It was the same year that Kozan Kato, a monk who had just spent more than four years in a solo retreat on Hazama Mountain, entered Eiheiji. Sawaki and Kato would later become lifelong friends. Sawaki officially left the Kangakuin at Horyuji that December and accepted a post as head of training (*tanto*) at Yosenji.

Kozan Kato met a monk by the name of Kanryo at Eiheiji,

---

* It should be noted further that while undoubtedly indebted to the *hongaku* (original enlightenment) thought of medieval Japan, Dogen's religion perhaps reflects certain sentiments—on the dark side of human psyche—akin to consciousness-only thought. [Hee-Jin Kim, *Dogen on Meditation and Thinking: A Reflection on His View of Zen* (Albany: State University of New York Press, 2006), 20.]

who, like Kato, had begun his training as a Soto Zen monk but switched to the Rinzai sect. Kato switched to Rinzai because the only severe training monasteries he'd heard about were Shogenji and Bairinji, both temples of the Rinzai sect. He went to Shogenji and found himself passing koans easily.* He had once studied as a lay student with Soen Shaku, and there too he passed koans without much effort. So he decided to just sit and skip *dokusan* (meeting with the teacher to check his koan practice). He was allowed to do this for his four remaining years at Shogenji and was respected for his determination to just sit. When they wanted to make Kato an officer at the monastery, he left early in the morning and never came back. From there he went to Hazama Mountain, living off the land and sitting his solo retreat for a few years. Here was an eccentric monk whose eccentricities appealed to Sawaki. When they met at Yosenji they soon became friends. Kato was the *tenzo* (monk in charge of the kitchen). He often went to the *tanto*'s room and they had long discussions. Among other things, they talked about how lazy the Yosenji monks were and how this monastery was not the right place for the two of them.

Kato's friend Kanryo had completed his Rinzai koan training and told Kozan that just solving a few koans was no way to judge the practice. "You have to follow it through to the end. Then, I promise that you will have a different attitude toward koan practice." Kanryo recommended Kato go to Bairinji and study under the master Sanshoken. "He's a special teacher," Kanryo said, "and you won't be disappointed."

* Koans are paradoxical statements that point to the nature of ultimate reality.

Sawaki and Kato joked a lot, enjoyed complaining about the weak-kneed monks at Yosenji, and felt a real connection with each other's serious approach to Zen practice. Kato, who arrived at Yosenji with nothing more than a *furoshiki* (a large handkerchief used to carry a few belongings), would look around at Sawaki's books, which filled the *tanto*'s room, and say, "If you promise to burn all these books, I'll follow you as your assistant for the rest of your life." Sawaki responded, "They cause me no problems." I haven't read anything about any discussions of their future practice plans, other than that they talked about possibly traveling together when they left Yosenji, though I can't imagine that they didn't talk about those future plans outside of traveling together.

One day they agreed to leave Yosenji. Before Sawaki could figure out exactly what he wanted to do, Kato was gone. He'd left the following morning, leaving a note for the assistant *tenzo*. Sawaki, who was known for his speediness, was later to remark, "That was the only time anyone ever left me behind." When they met years later, Kato told Sawaki that he left without informing his friend because "I thought you might be planning to have me carry half of your books."

Sawaki was thirty-four years old and Kato thirty-eight when they were at Yosenji. It was a pivotal time for both men in their religious studies. They were both to become exemplars of Zen practice, though each in his own unique way. As they progressed, their mutual love of zazen was skillfully transmitted to many of their followers. They immersed themselves in zazen, and that attitude was infectious.

For Kato, the progression was simple. He went to Bairinji

Monastery and during his first *Rohatsu sesshin*, his pride was literally knocked out of him.* He'd gone to Bairinji at age forty feeling he was a seasoned practitioner. But when the head monk sensed his conceit, he gave Kato so many whacks with the *keisaku* that the stick broke and went flying across the zendo. For Kato, it was a realization into his own arrogance and an awakening moment. He finally found a practice, though painful at first, that he felt an affinity for, and from then on he followed the Rinzai way taught at Bairinji.

For Sawaki, the process was not that straightforward. He certainly must have been influenced by Kato's story about spending more than four years in a solo retreat living in the mountains in a small hut practicing zazen most of the day.

. . .

During Sawaki's stay at Yosenji he took part in study and practice *sesshins* at other temples, meeting Sotan Oka, student of the famed Dogen scholar Bokusan Nishiari. Sawaki attended retreats run by Oka Roshi while he (Sawaki) was head of training at Yosenji. His relationship with Oka Roshi, though intermittent, lasted until Oka's death in 1921.

Kodo described Oka Roshi as a frightening looking character with deep-set eyes, a wide nose, and large mouth, and a powerful voice that was enough to intimidate students. This teacher

* A Rohatsu *sesshin* is a zazen retreat held in commemoration of the Buddha's enlightenment.

was very different from the gentle yet firm approach to Zen that Kato seemed to embody. Sawaki had little trouble accommodating both types of Zen men as he seemed to possess both qualities in his own person.

Sawaki describes Oka Roshi's one-on-one (*dokusan*) encounters with students that he overheard while sitting in the adjoining room at the time:

> First the monk sitting outside the *dokusan* room takes out his *zagu* [a mat for sitting] and spreads it in front of him, bows three times, and then enters the *dokusan* room. Soon his lips become dry and he feels choked up and words won't easily come. If it were someone easygoing like me [conducting the *dokusan*], it wouldn't be a problem. But with Oka Roshi and that frightening face of his, and on top of that, the way he stares with those deep-set eyes, most people would be scared out of their wits. "Well, what do you want?" Just hearing that in Oka's voice, there's not a person who wouldn't shrink submissively. A monk seeing Oka for *dokusan* would shrink that much more and his voice would be so faint one could barely hear it.

Then Sawaki gives an example: "'Tell me what the Great Matter is.' Roshi, without a moment's hesitation: 'Hmm, whose Great Matter?' Oka's response is blunt. 'Well, mine . . .' 'Yours? If it's yours alone, does it really matter? Ha, ha, ha.' I can still hear that laughter. Like the devil spewing his poison.

"I suffered many difficulties in my life since then," Sawaki goes on to say. "Many times I felt sad. Those times I always hear,

'Yours? If it is yours alone, does it really matter?' And that eerie laughter penetrates to the bottom of my ears."

. . .

To what degree Sawaki was influenced by his friend Kato's four-year solo retreat on Hazama Mountain we will never know. But after leaving Yosenji he approached his old teacher Rev. Saeki and asked for permission to do a solo retreat at Jofukuji, a dilapidated branch temple of Horyuji in Nara of which Saeki was nominally in charge. "If you are ever in need of a place to stay," Sawaki's old teacher had said to him, "just let me know."

Sawaki's father, Bunkichi, had died that year, relieving him of his financial responsibility, and he had temporarily given up on finding a sangha of serious students with whom to practice.

Jofukuji had been built on the property that had housed the famed Prince Shotoku (574–622). At the time Sawaki moved in, it had been abandoned for years. Few people knew it still stood. From Sawaki's point of view, it was perfect for his solo retreat. He spent close to three years at Jofukuji living on rice and pickles.

In Sawaki's words, "It was the perfect place for me. Here I would spend all my time practicing zazen." He said that the only people that came to visit him were Saeki, who brought him some pounded rice cakes and dried noodles, and one young Pure Land Buddhist student who wanted to practice with him. "He must have come to Jofukuji by mistake," Sawaki said, "because after rising at two in the morning to practice zazen for the first three days, he was gone."

Sawaki practiced from two in the morning until ten at night. As when he studied at Kangakuin, he ate rice and pickles and was thin and pale. During his stay at Jofukuji, Oka Roshi asked him to take time out to attend a *genzo* meeting at Eiheiji. Sawaki would be one of the assistant teachers during the weeklong meeting. If Sawaki thought that he'd finally arrived as a bona fide teacher, he was in for a surprise. He was scheduled to give two talks. He gave one during the first half of the week and was expected to give another during the second half. There was a tradition of the young monks having an eating contest halfway through the week. Though Sawaki was one of the teachers, he decided to take part in the contest. He hadn't yet completely come to grips with his competitive spirit, and he shocked the young monks with the drive to win, which he showed. One of the thinnest of the group, Sawaki ran away with the prize. He received a resounding round of applause by the other contestants.

The fact that Sawaki broke the contest record, having downed twenty-three bowls of bamboo shoot rice and eighteen bowls of tofu miso soup, turned out to be short-lived glory.* When he woke up the next morning, he had a severe stomachache. No doubt he remembered Fueoka's warning about running around without looking where he was going.

Sawaki was scheduled to give his second talk of the meeting that day, and he didn't intend to shirk his duty. When he arrived at the lecture hall, Oka Roshi took one look at the pale blue complexion on his star student's face and he called another

* I imagine the bowls were quite small, but still . . .

student, Hozen Hosotani, and whispered something in his ear. Hosotani left the room and came back a few minutes later. He walked over to Sawaki, took him by the arm, and led him out of the hall, and Oka stepped up to the platform to give an impromptu talk in his stead. Outside of the entrance to Eiheiji was a rickshaw waiting.

"The *genzoe* is over for you," Hosotani said, and he gave the rickshaw driver instructions on how to go to Jofukuji.

Kodo was later to say that of all the embarrassing moments of his life (and there were many), this was the most embarrassing of all.

. . .

From his time at Yosenji, Kodo had studied with Sotan Oka Roshi. He attended retreats when Oka was in charge, and with the exception of his embarrassing eating contest fiasco, they'd become close. Like Fueoka, his brother disciple of Nishiari, Oka seemed to respect students who demonstrated a lot of spunk when it came to studying the Way, and if the student sometimes went too far in expressing that energy, well, that was easier to deal with than lazy students. Hozen Hosotani, who was wild even by Sawaki's standards, was another of Oka Roshi's students. Sawaki and he quickly became friends.

Hosotani and Sawaki spent time together when Sawaki attended Oka Roshi's retreats, often assisting the roshi. Hosotani heard Sawaki give a talk once and said it was the first time he understood the text Sawaki was discussing. Sawaki referred to

Hosotani as the *wampaku tenzo*, which translates as naughty or mischievous kitchen chief.

Sotan Oka Roshi was asked to become abbot of Daijiji Monastery in Kumamoto Prefecture in Kyushu, a Soto Zen monastery that had a long history and was at one time the head Soto monastery of Kyushu, the southernmost of the four main islands of Japan. Oka Roshi apparently had no interest in leaving his temple on the Izu Peninsula, so he sent some monks from his temple to train at Daijiji and planned to have one of his longtime disciples, Hozen Hosotani, in charge of Daijiji in his stead. Hosotani, being his own man, said he wasn't interested. Oka Roshi wasn't someone who would easily give up. When he pushed him, Hosotani agreed to go to Daijiji only if it were to assist Kodo in running the monastery. Then Oka worked on Sawaki, telling him that it would only be a six-month position.

After his experience at Yosenji training monks who weren't interested in meditation, Sawaki probably lost interest in training monks. But six months seemed workable. He didn't realize that Oka was shrewd and managed to avoid Sawaki when the six months were up and it was time for Oka to take over. Sawaki ended up being in charge of Daijiji for over six years, until Oka Roshi's death.

Sawaki was pleasantly surprised to find the monks at Daijiji, many having been sent by Oka from his temple in Izu, willing to work hard and follow Sawaki's severe schedule. Sawaki said he could never have done it if Hosotani hadn't been encouraging everybody with his own enthusiasm. The two, Sawaki and Hosotani, worked as a team and helped restore the monastery to its lost glory.

. . .

During his six years in charge of Daijiji, Sawaki developed his own teaching philosophy. He met many people who would support him in this work for the rest of his life. One group of students who he considered to be essential in helping him clarify his own way of teaching were the students of the Fifth High School of Kumamoto. In his own words, "At Daijiji, because other [serious] monks came to practice zazen with me, I felt revived as a fellow devotee and as a teacher. What's more, the students of the Fifth High School of Kumamoto, whom I met when I was in charge of Daijiji, were one of the greatest influences in my life as a Zen practitioner."

For Sawaki, the energy and the inquiring minds of the students from the Fifth High School helped him develop a teaching style that was personal and devoid of technical explanations that would only make sense to those whose life study was devoted to Buddhist philosophy. These students were handpicked to attend one of the top high schools in the country, and they would eventually enter the Imperial University (which later on would be called the University of Tokyo) without taking any special entrance exam. They knew that they were special and walked around Kumamoto as if they owned the town. Their antics as they pushed their way into wherever they wanted to go was the attitude of a bunch of spoiled brats. For many of the citizens of Kumamoto, they were an arrogant group that belonged in reform school rather than a prestigious high school like the Fifth High School. For Sawaki, however, this was preferred to students whose low energy made severe Zen practice impossible.

One day the secretary of the Fifth High School Young Buddhist Club came to Daijiji to ask Sawaki if he would come and talk with the members. Kodo agreed, and it was the beginning of a relationship with the students that was both trying at times and educational beyond his imagination.

Sawaki describes the students as "walking along the central street in Kumamoto as if they were free from worldly cares with their high tooth wooden sandals, a rag-like towel hanging from their back pockets, their hair looking as though it had been through a mountain storm, and their stride as though they owned the streets."

One time a group of the high school boys were mingling in the center of town and one of them had to urinate, so he did it right in front of a *koban* (police box). A policeman came out and reprimanded him for his action. The group started to complain that he had to pee, so what could he do. The policeman got angry and took them all to the police station. They called the head of their dorm, who called the police captain, and they were all quickly released. It seems that the dorm head had a higher position in Kumamoto society, and the police captain had little choice but to let them go. It was that sense of their own privilege in the town that allowed them to act as if they owned it.

When Sawaki went to give his first talk at the high school,

he wore his black robe rolled up to his knees, his umbrella hat, his walking stick, and his sandals. He walked the eighteen kilometers at a speedy pace that defined him throughout his life. He arrived with sweat pouring down his face when he walked into the lecture hall. I don't believe these students had ever seen a visiting lecturer come looking as little concerned about his dress. They realized from the beginning that they weren't dealing with someone who they could easily intimidate.

Kodo Sawaki in monk's traveling umbrella hat and walking stick

Many people in Kumamoto, according to Sawaki, forgave these schoolboys their arrogant behavior because unlike other school students they expressed their feelings openly. Japan was entering a period known as the Taisho Democracy. It was the beginning of an era when people from a society that was authoritarian—where rules were strictly followed—were now experimenting with individual rights and democratic principles. For many of the citizens of Kumamoto, these students, though sometimes outrageous in their actions, were expressing themselves in ways the citizens themselves secretly envied.

The openness of the students helped open Sawaki to a larger world than the sheltered world of Zen to which he'd become accustomed. And he was direct in ways that were new to them, at least from someone who wore a Buddhist robe. It was for Sawaki a work in progress. On his first visit to the school, he opened with a question: "What remains with you boys if we take away your appetite for sex and food?" That really grabbed their attention. In Sawaki's words, "After that they listened like submissive puppies."

They followed him around when he gave talks elsewhere, often embarrassing him with their behavior. They didn't show the respect they showed Sawaki to the patrons at the places where he lectured. Though they did respect Sawaki, they didn't allow him to get away with explaining Buddhist theory unless the explanation was clear to them as laymen. When he tried to explain basic Buddhist principles to one of the students, Sawaki said, "I'd spent two or three hours explaining to Kusaba-kun, I believe it was Kusaba, the basic tenets of Buddhism. He listened quietly. 'Well,' I said, 'do you understand?' He made a sourpuss, cocked his head, and said, 'I didn't understand anything.'"

It was a frustrating moment for Sawaki, but it also encouraged him to learn to present Buddhist principles in ways that the average person would be able to understand. It was a quality that made his talks popular with persons of all walks of life—a signature of Kodo Sawaki's lectures throughout his career as a Zen teacher. He also came to realize that these high school students didn't particularly want to be spoon-fed. They appreciated a sincere attempt to explain things as long as the explanation wasn't hidden behind arcane Buddhist jargon. But they also liked to be challenged.

"'Osho-san, what is the benefit to practicing zazen?' The group asked me one day.

"'Even if you practice zazen, it comes to nothing.' My response seemed to shock them, and I wondered if it would resonate.

"'He's a gutsy priest!' one of them said. 'The pastor from the church would never say anything like that.' They grumbled as they returned to school. Then they showed up again: 'Osho-san, we've come to practice a zazen that will bring us no benefit.'"

From then on, a group of Fifth High School students came to Daijiji to practice zazen. They kept up with the monks, attending the severe *sesshin* schedule.

I don't know when Sawaki developed his "no-gain" zazen, but I suspect it was around the time he lived at Daijiji. His friend and assistant Hozen Hosotani understood it, and together they made its meaning clear to all the practitioners at Daijiji. After a few years helping Sawaki train the monks and lay students, Hozen

Hosotani suffered an appendicitis attack and had to return to his hometown. He never came back. By that time the schedule was solid and the practitioners didn't need to be pushed, so Sawaki had no resistance continuing the training routine. He found working with the monks, lay practitioners, and students of the Fifth High School at Daijiji very suitable to his temperament.

So when two families from branch temples of Daijiji asked Sawaki to ordain their sons, a twelve-year-old and an eleven-year-old, he probably felt like his perfect life was being challenged. What did he know about training youngsters? He trained his disciples the way he practiced himself—working them arduously. He wore himself out, too, to the point where he had to take time out at a hot spring every once in a while to recover his strength. But here were two young boys who never practiced Zen, who came to Daijiji because their parents asked them to.

Sawaki politely refused, telling them he was only caretaking Daijiji for Oka Roshi. They weren't easily discouraged. In Sawaki's words, "The parents felt that if their children were ordained by a disciple of Oka Roshi of Daijiji, it would be a plus when they made their way in the world. "No matter how many times I told them I don't have a temple of my own," he said, "they insisted I ordain their sons."

Sawaki eventually consented, naming the older one Shinko and the younger one Daiko. It was a new experience for him and a challenging one. "At the beginning, just a little thing would upset them and they would bawl. They missed their families," Sawaki said, not knowing how to deal with this new situation. He tried to calm them down, but really didn't have any experience with kids this age. Years later Sawaki attributed his problem in dealing with these boys to a lack of what in Zen is referred to as *robashin* (grandmotherly heart). He knew how to whip practitioners into shape, but didn't know what to do with young boys who were at the temple because their parents wanted them there, boys who had no desire to understand Buddhism. Though the clear reflection of his own weakness in this new situation came years later, it did help him recognize that a teacher needs more than just the ability to teach his students discipline. The teacher needs to be able to truly sympathize with his disciples on many different levels.

. . .

The monks, especially the ones Oka Roshi sent to Daijiji, and some of the students and a few of their teachers were okay with the severe schedule Sawaki set up for them, but it may not have satisfied some of the heads of the parish. They weren't as excited about a monastery where the practice was so all encompassing, leaving little time for them to enjoy temple life in a leisurely way. So when Oka Roshi died, Sawaki was asked to leave.

Fortunately, by that time Sawaki had developed a devoted following and some donated money, so he could rent a house and hold retreats there. The house he rented with the money he received from his followers was called Daitetsudo. The *tenzo* was a gourmet cook who freely spent money for ingredients to cook the meals, and there was no custom of giving money to the temple. Sawaki never charged for attendance at the retreats, and he printed pamphlets of the text he would use free of charge. So it wasn't surprising that the money he was given to continue his teaching wouldn't last long. One of the attendees to the regular retreats was quoted as saying some time after having to close Daitetsudo because the funds ran out, "I had always thought Rev. Sawaki was rich."

When that money ran out, a patron, Mr. Shibata, a member of the prefectural assembly, donated his second house on Mannichi Zan, a mountain near Kumamoto station, for Sawaki to live and continue to develop his practice. Some people joined Sawaki in morning zazen, and Kodo often traveled around the country conducting *sesshins* and giving Dharma talks. This was the beginning of Sawaki's "Moving Zendo" that was to last for twelve years. This was the genesis of a life on the road that would give him the epithet "Homeless Kodo."

. . .

One story that should be told before ending the Daijiji chapter in Kodo Sawaki's life is about a disciple named Akiko Takada. Sawaki's biographer, Tadao Tanaka, got this story from a man named Kokuo, who became a disciple of Sawaki during his Yosenji period. Kokuo became a teacher at an elementary school in Amakusa and would visit Sawaki at Daijiji during his school holidays. During the winter of the eighth year of Taisho (1919), Kokuo visited Sawaki. He entered his teacher's room and a woman of twenty-seven or twenty-eight came in with a tray of tea and sweets. In Kokuo's words, she was a small woman, dignified looking and beautiful. She was dressed in the appropriate Japanese dress and her skin was extremely pale. Sawaki introduced Kokuo to Akiko.

"This is my disciple Kokuo. We shared rice when I studied with Rev. Koho at Soshinji Monastery."*

Kokuo was treated as a guest at Daijiji that day. At dinner he found himself sitting opposite Akiko. They recited the *gokannoge*, the five prayers before meals, had a nourishing though thrifty Zen meal, and finished with tea. According to Kokuo's diary, he asked her in his direct Zen fashion, "You are young and are practicing in rather intimate circumstances with these young, vibrant monks on a daily basis. As a woman, are you aware that you are with the opposite sex?" She responded without a moment's hesitation, "Of course I am aware." Kokuo felt as if he were on the top of a peak and had fallen on his face. "How do you deal with that feeling?" he asked. Though it would be a rude question in other circumstances, it was not considered rude in the context of a Zen practice. "Clouds come and go with no mind. With me thoughts flow accordingly. At some point they disappear without my being aware." In his thirty years traveling and meeting many different people, he had never met anyone like her. He nodded, bowed to her, and went back to Sawaki's room.

"Well how was it? Did you have a feast?" Sawaki asked, curiosity reflected in his expression.

"I met her and had quite a feast. I'm referring to her response to my questions. She wasn't parroting anything she'd learned. I

---

* Meaning they roomed together at Soshinji.

just had a Zen encounter with a very special person. Tell me about this woman."

Sawaki proceeded to tell Kokuo about her. "That's Akiko Takada. She comes from a pretty wealthy merchant family in Osaka. After graduating from a girls' high school, she was stricken with spinal caries and was treated at Tezukayama Hospital. At that time her younger sister had just gotten married and visited her in the hospital dressed in her best clothes. Akiko felt a wave of loneliness because of her misfortune with her diseased body and started to move her heart toward Christ and the Buddha. I remember clearly what happened next."

Sawaki then continued to tell Akiko's story.

"At first she met with a Christian missionary. She listened to him and she read the Bible, but it didn't satisfy her or help with her spiritual crises. Then she heard about Nantembo Nakahara, a well-known Zen master whose intense approach to Zen was talked about throughout the country. He was a Rinzai teacher who resided at Kaiseiji Temple in Nishnomiya. Akiko attended his lectures and began to practice zazen. But here too there was something about the practice that didn't settle her spiritual agony, and also the physical suffering she felt continued."

Sawaki used to give lectures and conduct zazen practice meetings at an Obaku sect temple near Akiko's home. When she heard about the meetings, she decided to attend the lecture while sitting way in the back. Sawaki was lecturing on Keizan Zenji's *Zazen Yojinki* (A Record of Points to Watch in Zazen). She received a

kanbun text that Sawaki printed free of charge for his attendees.*
To Akiko, Sawaki looked like an arahat and his voice seemed to
come from deep down in his *hara* (lower abdomen).† She felt that
he spoke with an openness that came from the depth of his reality,
and it reverberated to the depth of her own spirit.

Akiko decided then and there to follow Sawaki and asked his
permission to go with him to Daijiji. The objections of her family
did no good. Once she made up her mind, she was determined
to go. Daijiji continued its severe practice schedule, and Akiko
followed it. She practiced with the monks and kept up with them,
never shrinking from any of the required activities. In fact, she
worked harder than many of the monks. She attended *sesshins* at
branch temples following all the rules of practice.

Akiko had gone to Daijiji in November 1918 and returned
to Osaka for the new year of 1920. Sawaki said he didn't know
whether it was the power of spiritual practice or the divine in-
tervention of the Buddhas and patriarchs, but her health had
improved considerably.

Tadao Tanaka wrote about an article from a newspaper in-
serted in Kokuo's notebook that announced Akiko's death and
talked about her practicing under Kodo Sawaki. When Sawaki
went to Osaka to conduct retreats, Akiko always attended them.
The article said that at one of the retreats, an influenza epidemic

* A *kanbun* is a Chinese characters modified to Japanese grammar.
† An arahat is an ideal of early Buddhism. In this case I believe she was referring to pictures of saints drawn and sculpted in temples.

spread and Akiko caught it. Tanaka, however, said that it was a mistake. Her spinal caries was the reason for her death. When Sawaki heard about her illness returning, he went to her house. Though she was not to receive visitors, when she heard it was her teacher, she rushed to greet him. He quietly returned with her to her bedside and sat beside her.

"How are you?" he asked.

She smiled faintly through her emaciated face. "I'm practicing for my death," she said and put her hands in prayer pose. "I have one request. This is the last time we will meet in this world. Can you bestow on me the Three Refuges?"

Sawaki immediately put his hands together and said, "Repeat after me, I take refuge in Buddha, I take refuge in the Dharma, I take refuge in the Sangha." When Akiko finished repeating after him, she continued sitting on her bed and quietly stopped breathing.

. . .

One wonders after reading this description of Akiko's relationship with Sawaki what effect this had on him and his practice. I found no other reflection by Sawaki about Akiko outside of his explanation to Kakuo. Since Sawaki had no difficulty talking on numerous occasions about the great effect the students of the Fifth High School had on his practice of Buddhism, his silence when it came to Akiko was surprising. Was the nature of Akiko's case more in the line of a faith-based reaction and not easily put in the form of how it impacts one's meditative practice of Buddhism?

Akiko seemed to have great faith in Sawaki and the Buddhism that came from his talks, and maybe that faith was more difficult for him to express in words.

The story of Akiko and her effect on Sawaki reminded me of a talk once given by Shunryu Suzuki in the middle of a *sesshin* at the Zen Center of Los Angeles. I had just come back from my first visit to Japan and spent the night with friends of a friend who were attending a Zen Center *sesshin*. It was sometime in late June 1969. I joined the group for a sitting, which was followed by a short talk by Suzuki. He had just come back from visiting one of his closest disciples, Trudy Dixon, who was in the hospital suffering from terminal cancer. What I remember from the talk was Suzuki saying Trudy was practicing zazen while on her deathbed. Trudy was the person who worked on Suzuki's *Zen Mind, Beginner's Mind*, dividing the sections according to emphasis and choosing the titles and epigraphs that follow the titles. She didn't live to see the book in print.

Suzuki said that he couldn't have imagined ever having a disciple like Trudy before coming to America. What struck me, and probably many fans of Suzuki, was the humanity he expressed when he talked about his personal feelings. I believe it was Suzuki's relationship with many American students who drew him out that added to the very personal way he gave his talks. He often said that a teacher hopes his students will go beyond him in their understanding of Zen.

What I sense from Kodo Sawaki from the time he was Saikichi, a wild kid from the slums of Ishinden fighting his way out of the chaos of his environment, is a series of learning situations mixed with some backsliding, and the Akiko relationship may have just been something he kept inside him, though he certainly learned from it.

. . .

After he was ordained as a monk at Soshinji in 1897, Sawaki was called Iron Pot because he was always bubbling with energy. Even his most revered teacher, Fueoka, couldn't slow him down.

So the next stage of his life on Mannichi Zan (Mannichi Mountain), the beginning of his "Moving Monastery," was fitting to him. His traveling around the country in response to invitations to conduct *sesshins* and give Dharma talks at temples, homes, and lecture halls turned this one trait into an asset. It also deepened his feeling for the necessity of doing zazen himself—a space where he could truly slow down.

According to Sawaki, Mr. Shibata, a member of the prefectural assembly, heard him read sutras at a memorial ceremony for the assassinated prime minister, Takashi Hara, and was taken by Sawaki's powerful voice. Though he was not a practitioner of Zen, Shibata must have felt something special from the way Sawaki recited the sutra and may have felt sympathy for the slain prime minister. Sawaki didn't express his feelings about the political situation in Japan at that time or about the slaying of the prime minister. But given that Hara was the first prime minister from the commoner class and a champion for the common Japanese, Mr. Shibata may have hoped that Sawaki, like himself, would be a champion for the average Japanese. The Prime

Minister was very likely assassinated because of his sympathy for the rights of the common Japanese. Shibata was aware of Hara's political positions and may have hoped Sawaki too would be a champion for the commoners. Shibata not only allowed Sawaki to live in his second home on Mannichi Zan, but also provided him with meals and allowed him to use the house for his Zen practice.

Sawaki lived by himself on Shibata's property, living alone as he describes it. He says that life alone on the mountain was the easy life. But when you scrutinize what he did during the twelve years he lived on Shibata's property, you realize that what was a leisurely life for Sawaki may have been a very busy life for most people. He described his life when he was not on the road as follows:

"When I am home, there is usually a group of people who come in the morning to do zazen with me. They gather at five-thirty, so I get up at four. I clean the house, burn incense, and change the flowers on the altar. Then I boil water for tea. By then the group shows up. I don't have help, so I do all the preparation myself."

The only person living near him was another monk, a Pure Land monk by the name of Donei Yokota, who lived on the next mountain, Hanaoku Yama. While Sawaki survived on the meals Shibata provided for him when he was home, and what his hosts gave him when he conducted retreats and gave lectures, Yokota lived off whatever people who visited the mountain for flower viewing or hiking had leftover. When Sawaki told him he'd just got back from Kagoshima, Osaka, and Sendai, Yokota described their different lifestyles: "You are a *quack quack* eater, and I'm a *donku kui*." Sawaki explained that the *quack quack* eater is a bird that goes here and there picking up food wherever he can find it, and *donku kui* is a frog that waits for some bugs to fly close to him and he snatches them with his tongue—without moving his body.

In the years Sawaki lived on Mannichi Zan, his reputation grew and he was invited to hold retreats and give talks all around the country. It began with visits to Saga Prefecture and throughout Kyushu. He traveled wearing the outfit of an itinerant monk.

"I gave a zazen meeting at Yoroin in Saga Prefecture when a priest from Seneiji Temple in Kurume approached me," Sawaki explained.

"'Sawaki Osho, I would like to hold a zazen meeting at my temple. The contributions I receive for funerals and memorial services are only enough to feed my wife and children. Could you come to my temple and conduct zazen meetings? We will treat you well and I will collect the participants.'

"Asking me without any embarrassment was intriguing. I was happy to accommodate someone who held back nothing, so I began holding monthly zazen meetings at Seneiji Temple."

The good treatment he was talking about turned out to be room, board, and a rickshaw ride to and from the Kurume station.

Seneiji was down the road from Bairinji, famously known as the "devil's monastery" because of the severe training the monks who trained there went through. On one of Sawaki's rickshaw rides to the station after a zazen meeting, he saw a monk walking toward him. The monk wore a ripped-up umbrella hat and looked to be about fifty years old.

"We recognized each other at once," Sawaki said.

"Hey."

"Hey."

"I hadn't seen Kozan in seventeen years," Sawaki said. "I hadn't seen him since we'd been at Yosenji in Matsuzaka in Ise. I'd heard that he was training at Bairinji, but never looked him up. Meeting him at this time was completely coincidental."

I'm sure they had much to talk about. For Sawaki, riding in style in a rickshaw was a bit of an embarrassment. The two monks used to rib each other when they were together at Yosenji, and they were both believers that monks who disregarded the vow of poverty were not monks in the true sense of the word. Kato used to tease Sawaki because he had so many books, and Sawaki admired Kato for showing up at Yosenji with only a small *furoshiki* scarf with the few essentials he needed (razor, toothbrush, and perhaps a change of underwear), and leaving the monastery with the same *furoshiki* scarf. As Sawaki sat in a high seat like some kind of royalty, he must have felt like he was caught again. It was always light ribbing and not of major importance to either of them.

After they were through catching up on seventeen years, they said goodbye. Kato and a couple of other Bairinji monks attended

Sawaki's zazen meetings at Seneiji from then on. It was not so unusual at that time for monks of one sect to attend retreats at a temple of another sect. In fact, the Seneiji priest had attended retreats at Bairinji when he was younger.

There couldn't have been a more unlikely pair of friends than these two monks. Sawaki had the gift of gab from the time he was a boy living at Ishinden. He grew up in a very poor neighborhood, and his adoptive parents threw away whatever little money they had on drink and gambling.

Kato was born into a moderately wealthy family before his father's business went down. But his father must have had enough money to get by, because he bought his son a temple (which was not so unusual in that area of Nagoya). Kozan Kato took his practice of Buddhism seriously, even though he had been given over to the temple against his will as a young boy. He practiced hard but was not comfortable giving talks.

Kodo Sawaki, on the other hand, found temple life an escape from an oppressive environment at home. He was happy to be there.

What the two friends had in common was a love of the practice of zazen. Though the zazen each practiced was distinctly different in approach, and they railed against the other's practice, they admired each other's commitment to sitting meditation.

That meeting on the road brought Sawaki and Kato together after the long separation, and they kept in touch from then on.

Kodo Sawaki (right) during his Mannichi Zan period
(Photograph courtesy of Daihorin Publishers)

. . .

During his stay at Mannichi Zan, Kodo traveled around Kumamoto and to Saga, Fukuoka, Kagoshima, and Nagasaki pre-

fectures. His straightforward Zen talk and his simple attire and generosity (he printed the texts he used at his talks and gave them to participants free of charge) made him a popular figure to believers in Buddhism regardless of sect. Sawaki even drew people who were not interested in Buddhism. The owner of the Mannichi Zan home, the prefecture assemblyman, for example, was not particularly interested in Buddhism. Mr. Shibata had a special feeling for Kodo Sawaki the man, and that was why he invited him to stay at the Shibata second home when he heard Sawaki had to leave his house, the Daitetsudo. Sawaki began getting requests to give talks and hold retreats in Tokyo, Osaka, Nagoya, and Sendai. He represented for many a return to the true spirit of monkhood.

The twelve-year period on Mannichi Zan was a period when Sawaki truly honed his teaching. He continued deepening his understanding of Dogen's Zen and probably lectured on various aspects of the *Shobogenzo*, though I can't find records of his talks during this period. He did lecture on the meaning of the authentic *okesa*, the shoulder cloth that is part of the habit of a Buddhist monk, symbolizing the patchwork robe.

I am limiting my study of Kodo Sawaki to his emphasis on zazen, because I feel that the practice he embraced more than any other is expressed in his unique pronouncement, "All of Buddhism is a footnote to zazen." I also feel that the practice saved him from himself. Like his trips to the hot baths when he was worn out from his strenuous teaching schedule at Daijiji, zazen is what brought him back to the quiet space in his mind that his traveling around the country, lecturing, and running retreats took from him.

One more thing that brought me to the conclusion that zazen or Zen meditation should be the focus of this book goes back to when I went to Japan to study Zen. Like most of the foreigners I met at and around Antaiji from 1969 until I left in 1977, I had come to temples in Japan to study meditation. For most of us, the study of Buddhism was second to the practice of Zen meditation. There were some, of course, who wanted to be members of the club, so to speak. But they were the exceptions. Kosho Uchiyama, the abbot of Antaiji, never encouraged any of the foreigners to become ordained, though a few did. The abbot was primarily interested in the foreigners that came to Antaiji to learn his teacher's form of zazen and hopefully take that understanding back to their countries.

For his Japanese disciples, Uchiyama realized that if they were to teach Sawaki's form of zazen, the best way was to become priests of their own temples, and that required credentials from a recognized teacher, i.e., to be ordained as monks. Before he retired from Antaiji, Uchiyama had his monks go to certified Soto Zen training temples. Because of its unique situation, having been opened for students to practice zazen, because it had no parish, and because of Sawaki's unique approach to simple meditation, Antaiji never became an official training temple. It did, however, become a hub for both monks and laypersons who wanted to study and practice zazen with no frills attached.

PART 2

The Teaching

Summer retreat at Teishoji Temple in Saku. On Sawaki's right in
the first row is Sodo Yokoyama, and Kosho Uchiyama is in row two
between Yokoyama and Sawaki.

When I researched the life of Sodo Yokoyama, the Grass Flute Zen Master, I learned that Yokoyama had corresponded with a man by the name of Shuseki Saito. Saito, a doctor of internal medicine and a pediatrician, was also an accomplished calligrapher and poet. He read and commented on Yokoyama's poetry and transcribed and edited his journals for publication. He was like an elder brother and advisor to the Grass Flute Zen Master.

As I read through some of Kodo Sawaki's talks, I noticed that the same Shuseki Saito had transcribed many of the talks that were delivered in Kumamoto City. Dr. Saito was a graduate of the Fifth High School in Kumamoto. He was born in 1883, making him three years younger than Sawaki, so he would have graduated by the time Sawaki had his memorable meeting with the students of the Fifth High School. He attended Sawaki's zazen meetings and lectures, following the roshi from his Daijiji period to Mannichi Zan and beyond.

Artist, healer, lover of the Japanese writing system, Saito employed his talents where useful but never flaunted them. He studied to be a doctor, and through his interest in Sawaki's teaching studied

Buddhism on the side. Putting writing and Buddhism together, he practiced shakyo, transcribing sutras. This was a common Buddhist practice. He was said to have reproduced the complete Lotus Sutra.

Dr. Saito transcribed many of Sawaki's talks when the master lectured in Kumamoto. Early on, when Sawaki noticed him writing out his talks, he would stop and point at Saito and say, "Don't write what I say!" Saito said he disregarded the admonitions and continued transcribing.

. . .

The following are translations of Shuseki Saito's transcriptions of Kodo Sawaki's talks in Kumamoto.

From a talk on the Heart Sutra delivered on August 15, 1942

Zazen is living the Dharma without confusion. You don't do things in a half-assed way. It is beyond thinking and non-thinking. When you settle into your position, you just hold it. That is your duty. The eye is the eye [working as the eye] and the navel is the navel. They do what they are there to do.

There is no difference in the ways of the ancients and the ways of today . . .

Each person practicing zazen, truly forgetting his self and settling into his position, working at eliminating delusion, will surely succeed.

"Beyond thinking and non-thinking" means nothing extra,

one with God, seamless with Buddha, just establishing yourself
correctly in your position and practicing there.

Sages have nothing [no-self]
No place they call their own.
They are one with heaven and earth
One with all things.*

. . .

Each of us should be positioned in "no-self." The duty that is fully
achieved in that position is where "no-self" exists. This is being
one with all things. It is the true teaching—the foundation of
heaven and earth. The one who works in this way is the Bodhisattva Avalokitesvara. Hence he works connected to the universe,
therefore having no hindrances . . . He throws out his self [ego]
and practices diligently in the duty of his station engaged in the
practice of deep Prajnaparamita . . .

Throw out the small you and the three thousand worlds will
all be your self.

. . .

From a talk given in August 1949 in Kumamoto

Soundless
Fragrantless

* This is a quote but I do not know its source.

Forever heaven and earth
Repeated—the unwritten sutra

—SONTOKU NINOMIYA

Statue of Sontoku Ninomiya

Everything in heaven and earth is an unwritten sutra. This is Ninomiya's greatness.* Sontoku Ninomiya was ahead of the pack.

* Sontoku Ninomiya was an agrarian reformer who helped improve agricultural techniques. His writing exalted rural life and earned him the affectionate title "Peasant Sage of Japan." Born to a poor family in 1787 in Sagami Province, he died in 1856. He was a moral leader who believed in the value of hard work and the dignity of manual labor. He instilled in peasants pride in their occupations, urging them to work to improve the general welfare of the poor.

When he was young, during his Kinjiro period, he was joyful when he lent and joyful when he borrowed.* Once he went to borrow a spade from a neighbor. The owner told him that he hadn't yet plowed his own field. Kinjiro said he would plow his neighbor's land, so the neighbor gladly lent him the spade.

He also helped rebuild the ruined homes in Sakura Village, working as a peasant laborer building homes for the homeless and encouraging other peasants to work hard.†

. . .

How many people know Taigu Ryokan, this eminent figure? Soma Gyofu critiques him as a literary figure only.‡ What a shame not to recognize Ryokan's Buddhism!

> If fleas and lice sounded
> Like the autumn insects
> My chest would be like
> The fields of Musashi no Hara.
>
> —TAIGU RYOKAN

This poem shows that Ryokan [thinks of] lice and fleas as his friends.

* Kinjiro was Sontoku's given name, so his childhood period was referred to as the Kinjiro period.

† It is not difficult to understand why Sawaki respected Sontoku. He took his monk's vow of poverty seriously, and though he had patrons from all classes, he taught the value of poverty through his own example.

‡ Soma Gyofu was a literary critic who wrote a book about Ryokan.

Statue of Zen Master Ryokan

A relative of Ryokan asked:
"Is there no way to avoid calamities?"
Ryokan's response:
"When you are met with a calamity, meet it completely. That is the wondrous Dharma of avoiding calamities."
Isn't that the wonderful working of this incantation?

Ryokan's farewell poem:

What shall I leave as a keepsake?
The cherry blossoms of spring,
The mountain warbler's song,
The crimson maple leaves of autumn.

[This is] the fullness of the universe. And zazen is the way to
see the original form of the universe in a day. Buddhism seeks this
original spirit. We see it in everything. That is our most important
aspiration.

. . .

From a talk titled "Dogen's Zen," delivered in August 1952 in
Kumamoto

I first came to Kumamoto on the fifth year of Taisho [1916] and
left on the tenth year of Showa [1935]. How much Zen still remains here in Higo?* As I talk in this hall tonight, I imagine
some whose grandmothers had brought them here [years ago] and
I wonder, unsure of myself, how many have had my Zen passed
onto them. If you understand Zen Master Dogen's Zen, if you
understand its truth, then my goal will have been fulfilled.

Dogen's Zen is *shikantaza*. It is not an idea. It means to
"just sit." [To quote the *Bendoho* (Rules for Practicing the Way)]

* The old name for the Kumamoto area.

"Standing out has no benefit. Being different from the community is not our way."

I'd studied the teachings for a long time and was shocked when I came across that statement. [Now I realize that] if we understand the statement, there will be peace in the world. In every society, people want to rush to be ahead of the group. I was a child from a poor family. I didn't graduate from elementary school. Then I became a priest who had *always* hated to lose. When I came across this [passage in the *Bendoho*], I felt crushed.

If we examine the Buddha Dharma carefully, there are *shura* [*asura*, demon], *gaki* [hungry ghosts], and *chikusho* [beasts], and no matter how [proficient] these three groups may be in tea ceremony, dance, etc., it is still the world of desire and sex. Then there is the desireless world of heavenly beings above the world of form. And you have to ascend even above that. You have to go beyond the cultural world. However, you will go back and forth returning to the culture of the lower realms of desire—so what can you do? There, to the extent you practice zazen, [you will have] the flesh and bones of the Buddhas and patriarchs. Other people will never turn you around. You will all live naturally; you will become yourselves. If you were born rich [or poor], that will be okay. That is what is called "dropping off." If you are an eighty-year-old grandma, you drop off mind and body as an eighty-year-old . . .

Though some recite the *nembutsu* [invoke the name of the Buddha] in order to go to heaven (or the Pure Land), for Shinran, reciting the *nembutsu* is irrespective of whether you go to heaven or hell. That is the meaning Dogen expressed as *shikantaza* [just sitting].

When you practice zazen you just sit. So what is the benefit? Here is a poem from Dogen:

Even without knowing, he protects the rice,
the scarecrow
in the mountain's small paddy
doesn't exist in vain

This is a reference to the monk Genpin Sozu, who left Mount Hiei in disappointment and went to a mountain in Nara to care for his fields.*

Genpin wrote the following poem:

The pathos of the monk
Caring for his mountain fields
The end of autumn
Nobody to talk with

No thinking, no enlightenment, complete as he is, a sake bottle and rain gear.

Nine hundred years ago there was a Zen system in which there were gradations of satori—three hundred and some tens of cases. Finally completing them all you would perfect a great satori. That system was contrasted with what was referred to as

---

* Sozu is the honorific title for a priest, bestowed by the emperor or government.

mokusho Zen [silent illumination]. It was also labeled *eko* and *hensho*.* The other teaching [which uses koans] was called *kanna* Zen.

Dogen Zenji's is a religion of practice. Dogen goes so far as to say there is no benefit in recitation with the mouth. In the *Bendowa*, Dogen wrote: "Continuously uttering sounds is like a frog crying in the night in a spring rice paddy and is ultimately worthless."

In the *Butsuyuikyogyo*, too, [the Buddha] warns against useless talk . . .† Satori is not something that is uncovered by the mind. Practice is enlightenment.

Again in the *Bendowa*, "A beginner's wholehearted practice of the Way is the totality of the original enlightenment." And in *Zanmai O Zanmai* [The King of Samadhi], "The posture for *shikantaza* is the most important meaning in Buddhist teaching."

. . .

It is easy to understand Kodo Sawaki's attraction to his disciple Sodo Yokoyama, the monk who was called a twentieth-century Ryokan. Sodo-san, as he was familiarly called, resembled the eighteenth-century Ryokan in his poetry, his delicate calligraphy, and his love of children, but in regard to his relationship with Sawaki, most important was how deeply he became absorbed in Sawaki's form of zazen.

After reading Dogen Zenji's *Zuimonki* (A Record of Things

---

* *Eko* and *hensho* mean "to direct light to illumine the source from which it comes."

† The *Butsuyuikyogyo* is a final instruction the Buddha gave his disciples.

Heard), Sodo-san started to practice zazen. After his father's death in 1937, Sodo-san participated in a zazen meeting at Sojiji Monastery, one of the two main Soto sect temples in Japan. There he heard a lecture by Kodo Sawaki, who by that time was a professor at Komazawa University and head of training at Sojiji Monastery. He asked Sawaki if he could be his disciple and was officially ordained the following year in Kyoto and given the Buddhist name Sodo. He was thirty-two years old.

Since Sawaki didn't have a temple—his epithet "Homeless Kodo" was something he was proud of—he sent Sodo-san to study with Eko Hashimoto Roshi at his temple in Izu in Shizuoka Prefecture. At age thirty-six, Sodo-san went to Kumamoto, where he practiced alone for four and a half years at a temple called Kaizoji. That was when he met Shuseki Saito and remained friends with him until Dr. Saito's death.

Sodo Yokoyama playing with children in the park

Like Ryokan, whom he looked up to as someone who justified a life of a monk living in a wood and practicing by himself, Sodo-san spent the last twenty-two years of his life sitting alone in a bamboo grove practicing zazen and playing music on a leaf. Like Ryokan, children flocked around him, enjoying his childlike nature.

Sodo-san collected his own poems and essays, and notes from Sawaki's lectures, and with the help of Shuseki Saito, put them together in a book he titled *The Wood Where I Stand* (我立つそま). I have taken the following quotes of Kodo Sawaki from *The Wood Where I Stand, The Grass Flute Zen Master,* and a book of Sodo-san's notes compiled by Rev. Joko Shibata, Sodo-san's sole disciple, titled *The Universal Posture of the Buddha* (普勧坐相みほとけ).

From The Grass Flute Zen Master

Practice zazen tenaciously and you are Buddha. Sawaki is always a deluded person. However, zazen seeps into Sawaki's blood drop by drop, making him a Buddha. How joyful!

. . .

Don't ever lose sight of impermanence. If you truly see impermanence, you are a Buddha with each exhale and a Buddha with each inhale. You have everything then and there. No reason to think about persevering in the future.

. . .

Zazen is not a competitive Way. You become yourself totally. Zazen is nothing more than becoming yourself.

You never feel that you can catch hold of zazen. You never chase after it and you never run from it. And it is nothing to fear.

. . .

No-gain is the most beautiful aspect of human beings. The aspiration of the Buddha and patriarchs is to throw away the aspirations of ordinary people.

. . .

Try practicing zazen believing you are Buddha and [you are practicing] Buddha's activity. Zazen will naturally become *shikantaza*. *Shikantaza* equals Dharma. Zazen is playing Buddha—the Buddha practices Buddha activity. That's what *shikantaza* is.

In whatever you do, if you do it with your whole self you will be that thing *as it is*.

. . .

The Buddha Way is the practice of zazen.

. . .

To practice zazen is to die.

Zazen is becoming a Buddha while you are a deluded person.

. . .

Zazen is not the way of the world. It is the way of the Buddhas and patriarchs. Which means zazen is renouncing the world.

. . .

Even though people become ordained, delusions don't disappear. However, when one does zazen, while delusions are there, the zazen posture is the posture of the Buddha. Hence zazen is the Buddha leaving delusions *as they are*.

Joko Shibata serving noodles to his teacher Sodo Yokoyama

From 普勧坐相みほとけ *(The Universal Posture of the Buddha),*
Sodo-san's notes of quotes from his teacher, Sawaki, transcribed
and published by his disciple, Joko Shibata.

Zazen is to be in tune with the vibrations of the universe. Then
you are the same as the Buddha.

· · ·

Zazen is the manifestation of the true form of the universe. And
one sees this manifestation [by practicing] zazen.

· · ·

Formless is just to be the form of a person being his self.

. . .

They say the Buddha Dharma is "to throw away delusion, embrace enlightenment, and separate from pain and gain comfort." In fact that is not so. The true Buddha Dharma is "not to be deluded by the past or enlightened by the present." That is to say, realize that there is no delusion and no satori.

It may be easy to satisfy yourself by living ambiguously, but it is taking the cheap way.

. . .

Though you may, for example, take pride [in your accomplishments], what meaning is it? Those who don't concern themselves [with recognition], who don't need anything, don't care about pride.

. . .

What if you are exhausted from pain and pleasure, from rising and sinking? Throw everything away and nothing will bother you.

There is nothing to grasp. Let go and the Way is there. Let go and your hands are full.

. . .

All the many relations go around and around.

. . .

Body and mind working as one is perfected in a moment. If it continues for one's whole life, it is Buddha.

Buddha Dharma is working moment by moment connecting mind and body. You can't say where it is. It's not a fixed thing.

. . .

Buddhist practice is not illumined by destiny. Contemplate the earth below the sun and moon and take no pride in the merit [of your contemplation].

. . .

We were not born simply because of karma. So we weren't born for a specific purpose.

Hey, you! Recognize that you are you and I am I. We are all fully complete. Each one of us is perfect.

. . .

Seeing outside of the ordinary is clarity. Separate from the worldly and enter the realm of joy.

. . .

Buddha Dharma is the manifestation of the oneness of mind and body. The oneness of mind and body means "practice and enlightenment are one."

In our teaching, the most important thing is for the body to realize the Self.

. . .

Do not seek after the truth. Only cease to hold opinions.* Opinions are arbitrary. Zazen means to die. You cease to have opinions. You become completely zazen.

. . .

Faith-mind means believing in the Unchangeable Truth, or Eternal Truth, which means putting a stop to human thinking.

---

* This is a quote from *Shinjinmei* (Believing in Mind), a short piece attributed to the third patriarch, Seng-ts'an (Sosan in Japanese). It is one of the earliest Ch'an (Zen) writings and shows a strong Taoist influence.

*Two are derived from One; but do not even cling to the One.** One means the Dharma. One is the life of teacher and disciple.

. . .

Nagarjuna's *face of the full moon* is zazen.† It is the seamlessness of delusion and satori, and no beginning and no end. That is the *face of the full moon*. This *face of the full moon* is to deluded people the feeling of being incomplete.

. . .

The manifestation of the face of Buddha Nature expresses the body of all Buddhas. It is an expression glorifying zazen.

---

* This quote is from *Shinjinmei* (Believing in Mind).
† This phrase is taken from the "Buddha Nature" chapter of the *Shobogenzo.*

The *face of the full moon* is the Buddha without any borders, or ordinary people without any borders. Hence it is the form of zazen without borders.

. . .

Zazen is the form where Buddha Nature dwells, and it is the work of Buddha Nature.

. . .

The Buddha is where human thoughts disappear. Birth and death are no more, likes and dislikes disappear; whatever *is* is fine. The ideal of this is zazen.

When you do zazen, you become a first-class human being.

. . .

Zazen is the Buddha doing what Buddhas do.

To know that you are bad is preferable.*

. . .

Zazen is colorless and transparent, so deluded thoughts and ideas become very clear to you.

. . .

Zazen makes things clear, when at other times they are deluded.

* Preferable to being bad and unaware of it.

A shadowless tree and a witherless flower together make up the life [of nirvana].

. . .

In this wonderful art of freedom from ignorance, affliction, pain, and delusion, you become a deathless person and [hence] unborn.

. . .

This body is used for the sake of zazen—it clarifies the important matter of causes and conditions [i.e., life].*

* Yokoyama's note to this phrase: "This means that there is no you [ego], so it is natural that this means a zazen that gives you nothing. It is *shikantaza*."

It's okay not to have satori. Just don't delude yourself.

. . .

Not to clarify the Self is not to realize that you are Buddha *as you are*. That is blasphemy of the Self.

. . .

I have been Buddha since the distant past. The Buddha came to this world to inform us of his original vow [to save all sentient beings].*

---

* This is from the teaching of the Pure Land schools of Buddhism. Sawaki was strongly influenced by these schools.

Zazen is the marker [code] for the Buddha since the distant past.

. . .

Though there are radio waves, without a radio we can't receive them. Even if we have a radio, if the wave frequency is not in harmony with the radio, we won't be able to hear it. Zazen too must be done within [the frequency of] Buddha Nature. It has to be done correctly or Buddha Nature will not be clarified.

. . .

Infinite Light. I want zazen to be clear [transparent] and colorless.*

---

* Yokoyama interprets this as wanting to practice zazen that is non-thinking, non-imagining.

You don't need anything to practice zazen; you don't need a pen or a notebook. You don't need satori and you don't need delusion. You don't need to bring anything with you. People can't comprehend this, thinking it's too broad and limitless.

. . .

Zazen advances beyond the highest satori.

. . .

Zazen is to arrive at the ultimate place. The Buddha Way is the practice of zazen. Hence one's faith that the zazen form is Buddha. Buddha is non-thinking, and the zazen form is this non-thinking.

To sit zazen, just sitting is enough. [Then] zazen becomes zazen.

. . .

People want to put satori in a box, like a little garden box. If it can be put in a box, it is no longer Buddha Dharma.

. . .

Don't forget to contemplate impermanence. Contemplate it on the out-breath respecting Buddha, and on the in-breath respecting Buddha. That is everything at that time and in that place only. There is no reason to consider any other effort.

Shakamuni Buddha came back from begging barefoot, washed his feet and took his meal. He spread his mat and sat and gave a sermon. At that time Sharihotsu kneeled by his side, exposed his right shoulder and asked the Buddha questions.* This was stated in the Agama Sutras. The Buddha didn't ask for money; he just spoke. The sermon was free. Because it was free, it was respected. Being a monk doesn't cost anything, and that's pretty good.

. . .

"*Practice of peace and happiness.*" Do what you are supposed to do. Don't do what you are not supposed to do. Peace and happiness come from applying as much [energy] as possible to what you do. That is the key.

. . .

Zazen does not teach one to win over others. You become yourself [completely]. Zazen is about you only.†

* This was the formal custom of the time.
† Yokoyama explains that this does not mean to be selfish. We are all the one Self.

[With zazen] you become yourself, completely leaving delusions as they are. The place where you become yourself completely is where you attain Buddhahood. This is where the Buddha Dharma is.

. . .

You can't see your true Self. [But] you can become it. Becoming your true Self is zazen.

. . .

Human beings have the desire to understand things. This can be trouble.

Each of us with our body *as it is* is above discriminatory thought, walks alone through the universe, and is an independent being. That is the true religious point of view—religious practice is right here.

. . .

Zazen is not something you feel you've grasped. There's nothing to chase after, there's nothing to run away from, and there's nothing to fear.

. . .

If you think you are going to die, that's fine. Whatever happens, if you intend to die, go ahead.*

. . .

No-gain—This is the most beautiful aspect of human beings.

---

* Yokoyama interprets this as seeing everything as no-thought, no-delusions.

In April 1935, at the request of the president of Komazawa University, the major Soto Zen sect university in Japan, Kodo Sawaki became a professor of Zen studies. The following December he was appointed instructor of apprentice monks at Sojiji Monastery, one of the two major Soto Zen monasteries in the country.

In June 1937, Sodo Yokoyama attended a summer Zen study period, and the following year Sawaki ordained him. In July 1941, his younger brother disciple, Kosho Uchiyama, attended a Sawaki lecture at Sojiji and was ordained by the master the following December.

In 1921, a layperson who wanted to encourage scholars and teachers of Soto Zen had invited Sotan Oka Roshi to be founding abbot of Antaiji. The temple was to serve as a study monastery. Oka Roshi became ill soon after the opening ceremony. A number of Soto teachers trained there, but during World War II funds were withdrawn from the Antaiji project.

In 1949, Kodo Sawaki asked Rev. Sokuo Eto, the abbot at that time, if his disciples could stay there and practice. Eventually Sawaki became the fifth abbot of Antaiji in name while continuing to teach at Komazawa University and travel throughout Japan. He visited Antaiji once a month to conduct *sesshins*; he put his disciple Kosho Uchiyama as caretaker while he was on the road. Uchiyama stayed at Antaiji, and with other disciples took care of his teacher when Sawaki's legs failed him. Sawaki was confined to the temple from 1963 until his death in 1965.

Kosho Uchiyama became the sixth abbot of Antaiji after his teacher's death. More than any other, Uchiyama, through his writing and position as abbot of Antaiji, was responsible for spreading Kodo Sawaki's teaching to the Japanese- and English-speaking world.

The following excerpts are from translations from a book Uchiyama wrote titled *Yadonashi Hokusan* 宿なし法句参 (The Dharma of Homeless Kodo). The book was assembled from a series of articles Uchiyama wrote for the *Asahi Newspaper*. It was translated by Uchiyama's disciple Koshi Ichida with the help of Marshall Mittnick and later edited and translated by Okumura Shohaku and George Varvares.* My translations are from the 1971 publication by Hakujusha.

. . .

A fellow once said, "I wasted my whole life practicing zazen."

. . .

Each and every one of us has to live out the life of his or her self. There is no need to compare who's better looking or who's smarter.

. . .

Sit resolutely where being superior or inferior doesn't matter.

---

* I have only included excerpts of Kodo Sawaki's words. For Uchiyama and Okumura's comments, see Kosho Uchiyama and Shohaku Okumura, *The Zen Teaching of Homeless Kodo*, ed. Molly Delight Whitehead (Boston: Wisdom Publications, 2014).

A monk should be a person who creates a life of the Self.*

. . .

Comfort and joy in this world eventually turn into suffering and pain. It is only a limited comfort and joy. The fortunes of this world will turn into misfortune—that is the only kind of fortune there is.

. . .

The present educational system is no good. Students are tested and graded and given a number. How stupid! What is superior, what is inferior? If someone has a good memory, is that person considered superior? Is one inferior if he has a bad memory? How many silly people have good memories?

. . .

If a person gets poor grades, he might feel inferior for the rest of his life. How foolish it is to give someone an inferiority complex.

. . .

* I use a capital S for "self" when I believe Sawaki is referring to the universal self.

The original aim of education was to find meaning in life. After the Meiji Revolution, however, school became merely a means of getting a good job.

It's not so bad when people are alone, but when they become a part of a group, paralysis sets in. They become quite foolish and can't tell right from wrong. It is truly "group paralysis." There are even people who pay a membership fee to be a part of this foolishness. Some take great pains to spread the word to intoxicate others.

We have to stay away from these societies in order to prevent this paralysis. Zazen is the way we say bye-bye to this foolishness.

. . .

Our practice of zazen is to hibernate and see the world with a fresh perspective. However we look at it, practicing zazen is the best. When we do other things, too often it is the work of a demon.

What is the true Self? Rather than being a blank sheet, it is brilliantly transparent like the blue sky, in which all sentient beings are connected.

. . .

The most important aspect of religion is how we live our everyday lives.

. . .

People reading the same newspaper read different sections: Some go first to the stock market section. Some go to the sports section. Others read the serialized novels. Still others go to the political section. Each one has a different interest. People look at newspapers in accord with their discriminating thoughts.

When they view things according to their thinking, they will all see things differently. When they do not see things through their discriminating thinking, they will recognize their commonality. However, humans think and think and as a result make mistakes.

To study Buddhism is to study loss. The Buddha is a good example. He gave up his kingdom, his beautiful wife, and his son, discarded his splendid clothing for dirty garments, and spent his life traveling barefoot and begging for his food. All the Buddhas and ancestors suffer loss intentionally.

Monks who want to make their way in society are making a mistake. We are nothing more than beggars through and through.

. . .

Zazen is like reentering our mother's womb. It is not work.

. . .

We don't practice to attain satori. We practice being dragged here and there by satori.

We are glared at by zazen, scolded by zazen, obstructed by zazen, dragged around by zazen, and spend our lives in tears. How fortunate we are!

. . .

All-knowing wisdom is to realize that there are no cracks through which we will slip from Buddhahood. The night train carries us even when we are asleep.

. . .

A religious life means you reflect on yourself and always study your life.

The more conscious we are, the more we realize how trivial we can be.

. . .

Shikantaza [just sitting] is the highest place we ordinary human beings can reach in this body of ours.

. . .

When husband and wife quarrel, neither of them can see the delusions in their thinking. However, if they practice zazen, they will realize that their arguments are based on misconceptions.

. . .

What will zazen do for you? Nothing! Until you hear this so much that calluses form on your ears, until you truly understand and just practice, it will really amount to nothing.

. . .

One of the appeals of Zen Master Dogen is that he sees the Buddha Dharma as the Self. He doesn't see it as a fairy tale for ordinary people.

. . .

When we are healthy, we forget about our bodies. While our legs are strong, we walk and run and don't give a thought to them. These days I think about my legs because they are weak . . . We usually concern ourselves with things when they give us problems. Otherwise we don't give them a thought.

Some say they don't feel anything special in my talks. That's true. There is nothing special about me. The Buddha Dharma simply invites us to a place where nothing is special.

. . .

People mistake the faith-mind for some kind of ecstasy. The type of ecstasy they welcome is fantasy. When we sober up from this type of ecstasy, we call it faith-mind.

. . .

"Theory of Consciousness Only" separates consciousness into subject (I) and object (world).* Within this structure, we chase after objects or run from them, creating a big fuss. Delusive desires are strange!

---

* Sawaki studied this theory as a student in the Nara Kangakuin.

We often say, "I saw it with my own eyes" and "I heard it with my own ears." Though we say it as though it is fact, we have to question our eyes, ears, tongue, body, and thoughts. We say we are happy or we are unhappy, but these are merely thoughts. The truth is it's all nothing special.

. . .

Everybody is in his or her own dream. The discrepancies that exist among these dreams *are* the problem.

. . .

We say "reality, reality," but all are dreams. The only reality is the reality in a dream.

. . .

People are shocked by revolutions and wars. However, they are struggles within a dream. After you die, you will view it and realize it was all a dream.

. . .

What I call "me" cannot sustain itself [by itself]. When we give up this "me," it becomes the Self that is the universe.

Heaven and earth give. Air, water, plants, animals, and human beings give. All give to each other. We live within this circle of mutual giving. Whether we are grateful or not, it's a fact.

. .

Without demanding "Give it to me!" the world in which we give and receive, different from the world in which we snatch things for ourselves, is beautiful. It's a vast and boundless world.

. . .

The one attitude to have and demonstrate in the ten directions is "don't covet anything." There's no greater offering than this.

Zazen is the way to connect with the whole universe.

. .

Samadhi is practicing with all your heart every moment in accord with the entire universe.

. .

Satori isn't arriving at a special place that is difficult to reach; it is simply being natural.

. . .

Because all is the content of the Self, we have to act considering what others feel.

The true Self is that which does not think of itself only as "me."

. . .

The root source of delusion is the "me" thought, which is secondary [to who we are].

. . .

The real state of things is [inherently] taken care of. There's no need to twist things into what we want.

No matter how much you suffer in the transitory world, it won't enrich your life. But if you accept that world as the content of your zazen, the Buddhist teachings as well as your life will be enriched.

. . .

Zazen is not something we can store up. Saint Shinran too rejected the idea of storing up *nembutsu*. That's why Shin Buddhists call storing up religious practice "self-power" [and reject it].*

. . .

Amida Buddha says, "Don't worry, everything is okay. No sentient being is forever lost in delusion. Relax!" Still, ordinary people say, "Oh, no, this is terrible!" and whimper and cry.

. . .

People make a big fuss about being happy, being important, being liked, and being good. The world beyond discrimination, [in Dogen's words] *hishiryo*, is letting go of human thought.

. . .

---

* Shin Buddhists think that "other power" is the Way. They feel that using "self-power" is a rejection of "other power" (or Amida's vow) and disregarding Shinran's realization.

Buddhism is realized through practice; we understand it through the body. We must practice zazen and have the proper control of our muscles. With zazen as our standard, we train ourselves in the proper attitude toward life. This practice will enrich your life [and bring you] peace of mind. Generally speaking, practice should be your approach to life.

Fundamentally, we can walk in any direction: east, west, south, or north—whichever way we wish. Each and every activity permeates the entire ten-direction world. We simply practice manifesting eternity through our action in each moment.

. . .

Once Sen no Rikyu needed a carpenter to drive a nail into an ornamental alcove post in a teahouse.* After looking here and there, Rikyu decided on the best spot. The carpenter marked the spot and then took a break. Afterward, he couldn't find the tiny mark. He asked Rikyu to search again for the best location. After a while, the tea master decided on the spot and indicated it to the carpenter, "Right there!" When the carpenter looked carefully, he found it was the very place he had marked the first time. You see there is always a clear aim right in the midst of emptiness—emptiness where nothing is fixed.

. . .

The truth of Buddhism is realized only through practice; it is attained through the body. The way we use our muscles must be in accordance with zazen. Practicing zazen, we develop an attitude toward life in each and every activity. This is practice. Within it, we actualize true peace of mind.

* Sen no Rikyu was the father of the tea ceremony.

. . .

To practice the Buddha Way is to become a person who will never die, who is not at all different from the Buddha pervading the universe forever.

Kosho Uchiyama often said that after studying with Sawaki for twenty-five years he couldn't say whether the words he used in his talks were his or his teacher's. That statement encouraged many of us who trained at Antaiji to want to study the words of Kodo Sawaki. A great many Americans have come into contact with the teaching of Sawaki through the translations of two Antaiji monks, the late Rev. Koshi Ichida and Rev. Shohaku Okumura. They were aided in their translations by Marshall Mittnick and the late George Varvares. Without the pioneering work of these four men, few Americans would know the unique teaching of this iconoclastic Zen teacher.

In Japan, however, Kodo Sawaki is well known throughout the Zen world. There are over twenty volumes of his talks published by Daihorin Publishers. For a while, most of those books went out of print, and only recently has Daihorin republished them.

Since Sawaki traveled the country speaking wherever a request was made (up until the last two years of his life), many who may never have read his printed lectures knew this man through his dynamic and entertaining talks. I am reminded of the seventeenth-century Zen teacher Bankei Yotoku who preached a Zen throughout Japan that reached people of all walks of life and all levels of education.

I fear that Sawaki may have been the last of this type of Zen teacher. Thanks to the work of Kosho Uchiyama and his disciples, we at least have a written record of Kodo Sawaki's teaching in English.

When Uchiyama retired from Antaiji, his disciples moved to different parts of Japan and some to America. The Rev. Shusoku Kushiya moved into a house near where Uchiyama and his wife Keiko had retired in a village outside Kyoto called Ujidawara, serving his teacher in any way he could. Kushiya loved literature and kept copious notes of his teacher's talks whenever possible. He edited many of Uchiyama's sayings about Sawaki, as well as the lectures the abbot gave after his retirement, and he published them through Daihorin Publishers. He also published a regular booklet with contributions of many people connected with Uchiyama and Sawaki, called "Tomo Ni Sodatsu" (Learning to Grow Together).

The following are excerpts from a collection of quotes by Sawaki in a book Kushiya published titled *Sawaki Kodo: Ikiru Chikara To Shite No Zen* 生きる力としての*Zen* (The Living Zen of Kodo Sawaki).

. . .

Selfing*

It's not a good thing to continue as we've done up to now. We have to renew ourselves this year. We have to renew ourselves each month. We have to renew ourselves each day.

. . .

Start each day with an everlasting now and an always here. This limitless moment is the new fact of living in the present. The past when you consider it in the present is a new past.

. . .

Practice zazen today. Do it now as if for the first time since your birth, and become completely new, like a feeling of a fresh New Year, a New Year zazen. Every day you welcome in the New Year. That is joyful. Our true practice is to give birth to this New Year every moment.

---

* "Selfing" is not a word, but Rev. Kushiya seems to use the noun "self" as a verb, giving it the sense that Sawaki used.

There are those who worry on their day of ordination: "Oh boy, now I'm a monk, but will I be able to pass through my whole life as one?" That kind of worry is unnecessary. Be a monk for that day only. Live each day as a monk for that day only.

. . .

Start each day as if you were born that day. Always make every day your first.

. . .

Even at this age, I do zazen with a beginner's mind. If you become accustomed to zazen, it becomes false zazen. Get used to it and it isn't worth a shit. You have to do it fresh every time. That's why the most important time is when you awaken that beginner's mind. Don't ever think you have mastered zazen just because you've become familiar with it.

Always practice as a beginner. You are closest to that feeling when you enter the meditation hall full of apprehension. Don't forget that first time you practiced zazen—become an amateur.

. . .

Zazen is not something a person will become better at as they get older. While you are practicing, that is zazen. So whether your practice is going well or poorly, you must always return to practice.

. . .

You cannot say, "Now I've seen the Buddha" [and that's it]. We have to see the Buddha anew all the time. We have to listen to a fresh discourse. What part of the Buddha's limitless Dharma are we hearing? There is Buddha teaching in Marxism. We can hear it in the words of Engels. Don't overlook the Buddha anywhere.

The Buddha gives life sustained by Mother Nature; in other words, living according to the truth of the universe. During our lives in this body, we are not sustained each moment by our own effort. [Yet] we continue moment after moment without any rest. That is what is meant by "the original face." The Buddha continuously gives life to this original face without our effort. Hence, the Buddha never rests.*

. . .

There is a major contradiction between the terms "Instantaneous Birth and Death" and "the Clarity of Cause and Effect." The former means what was before does not become that which is now, and what happens later on does not come from the present. Yet today's waste was yesterday's meal, which is clearly cause and effect. If you eat a lot of meat and onions, no matter how much you try to hide it, your pee will stink. This means today is a continuation of yesterday and tomorrow is a continuation of today. However, according to "Instantaneous Birth and Death," everything is always new. No matter how much you try to understand this contradiction with your rational mind, its limitless reality cannot be clarified. However, if you don't try to attack it [with your mind] but rather embrace it with non-thinking, that is called the "Direct Leap to the Ground of Buddha."†

* Here again, Pure Land Buddhism shows its influence in Sawaki's teaching.
† "Direct Leap to the Ground of Buddha" is from *Shodoka* (Song of Enlightenment).

. . .

New plums blossom from old stalks. Forever the new comes from the old—it mixes with the old. That is the highest meaning of the Buddha Way.

To aspire to learn [Buddhism] means to aspire to follow the Way. To follow the Way means to investigate your self. You can't expect to find the path if you leave this human life out [of the picture]. It is here where one learns how to live his life—in other words, becomes a student of the Way.

. . .

When religion becomes organized it deteriorates. You [should] just practice [yourself].

. . .

If you ask what exactly it is that the Buddha taught: He taught each one of us to know the Self, to study the Self, and he taught us to know what each one of us should do here and now.

I don't stand here giving talks for others. I give them for myself. You [should] not listen to *my* talk, but rather listen by stirring up something inside you, something that stirs *you* and pulls on you; it should truly call to you. That is what these talks should be. It's not as if you can get something from someone or give something to someone.

. . .

(To borrow Saint Honen's words) . . . therefore you shouldn't show off [your knowledge] of the Buddha Way, or treat it like a salable product. You should recite the *nembutsu* like a robber, [even] hiding it from your wife and child.

. . .

Zazen is not easily spread because it is not something you show off, but rather a practice in which you just sit. You must practice zazen as if you were doing the worst thing possible.*

---

* Sawaki may be exaggerating a bit, but he wants to bring home that zazen is done for zazen's sake and not something we do for personal gain.

Even though you desire to develop the "Way-Seeking Mind" and listen to the Buddhist teachings and rid yourself of things you don't need, if you do that without being attentive enough, it all becomes another kind of merchandise.

. . .

If you don't try to better yourself daily, you will easily be led astray. If you don't cultivate your practice daily, it will rust. So here you must not lose track of your true Self, and [you must] attain Buddhahood every day. You have to approach your food as if you were attaining Buddhahood. In all situations, never lose sight of the true Self.

. . .

Impermanence is this very instant *as it is.* You win or lose this moment and . . . finished. Every day you breathe out and breathe in and that's it. And that should be the end of it. However, we attach to things and delude ourselves. If we have children, we think of ourselves as parents. If we have grandchildren, we think of ourselves as grandparents . . . The grandchild is the grandchild, period. The grandparent is the grandparent, period. The child is the child, period. Here we see for the first time the flavorless, colorless reality of the sole universe.

These days, people feel dissatisfied. It's because the modern man feels he is unexciting and that he must do something about it. And he thinks he *can* do something about it. That is what we call delusion. There is no other self than the one who lives with these thoughts right now. It is the self that can't be replaced. There is no place where another *me* is. So the thoughts and activities of our selves today are irreplaceable. [Hence this self] must be the true Self.

. . .

In our lifetime we must grab hold of the true Self. We have to discover our true purpose. Arriving at this true Self is what we call enlightenment. Truly seeing ourselves, keeping our feet firmly planted on the ground, we walk this way without losing sight of who we are. That is attaining the Way.

. . .

The Self, *as it is*, is identical to Buddha Nature. So when you say "I am dull" or "I am no good," you are dishonoring the Self. It's important that you get hold of Self, stay with it, and understand it. You will have peace of mind if your daughter is your daughter and your wife is your wife. Your daughter is *only* your daughter and your wife is *only* your wife. That is the manifestation of Buddha Nature.

Group mindlessness settles in and you can't tell black from white. Whatever wrong you do, if you do it with a group, you don't feel it is wrong. Because of this group mindlessness, you will at some point lose sight of the Self. Remember! Be your self!

. . .

True peace of mind comes when you show a strong concern [for your action] and make every effort not to lose sight of the Self. Step by step, act deliberately, keeping your feet planted firmly on the ground—then you will finally have peace of mind.

. . .

Peace of mind as a general expression could be nothing more than a fabrication of peace of mind. Because one chases after that kind of [so-called] peace of mind, it [in fact] becomes a restless mind. Shinran too threw out a *nembutsu* in which one accumulates [merit from] many recitations. He called this accumulation of religious practice [pejoratively] a "self-powered tendency." Practicing while having an uneasy mind will result in a peaceful mind. The interplay within the peaceful and uneasy minds is the mind of great peace.

Though children can be spurred on and cajoled into studying, and receive praise from others, they know nothing about themselves. Real substance of themselves is ignored. In order to grab hold of religious practice or Zen, even if you care little for God or have lost faith in Buddha, if you hold fast to the substance of your self, become your self, you will become a complete person.

. . .

To live in solitude is to live in peace. Where does one live in peace? In the Self. We live in peace within the life of the Self. There we are not directed by things. We don't operate according to delusive thoughts, nor do we operate according to our attachment to Buddha or Dharma. We are not moved by anything [outside our selves].

. . .

We shouldn't do things for personal gain. In our lives we have to polish tiles.* A life in which we don't seek benefit is our daily devotion.

---

* Referring to a koan where Nangaku criticizes Baso for practicing zazen with the intention of being enlightened. Nangaku starts to polish a tile in order to make a jewel—showing his disciple that no amount of polishing will ever make a jewel. Sawaki's take on this is contrary to many. He says we should polish the tile, but just to do it, not to be enlightened.

A religious life is one where you have an exemplary attitude when nobody is around to see you. We have to be transparent. We have to be clear about ourselves. We have to follow the true Way even when others don't see us.

. . .

I'm always scolding myself. Scolding may sound strange; I mean looking at myself. *Ekou henshou*—"to direct the light back to illumine the source from which it comes." As long as I keep an eye on myself, I'll be okay.

. . .

Ekou henshou means you are shown who you are—you are sitting quietly and observing. You are watching yourself as if you are watching a movie. As you watch yourself, you will understand *shujo*—ordinary people or sentient beings. You will understand that you are none other than a deluded ordinary being.

Transmitting the teachings means transmitting yourself. You become yourself.

. . .

That the Buddha was a great man who lived many years ago and was written about in sutras doesn't mean a thing. It is your problems that must be understood. Practice is what you do about your problems.

. . .

No matter how great Dogen Zenji was and no matter how erudite his talks were, they are not you. That kind of outside stuff is discrimination, delusion, sleep talk. Here and now, where you are, separate from the discriminating mind, that is what we call *fukeron* [refrain from meaningless discussion].

A deluded lump of cells I call me can express itself just like the Buddha. That's because of zazen. Zazen creates the highest form of a patriarch I call me.

. . .

The Buddha is me, myself. There is no other Buddha than me.

. . .

Though we think we live as individuals, in fact, we are given life by Mother Nature. We are not alone. We are a universal truth. The universal truth we call the Self is referred to as *jin jippou kai shinjitsu nin tai*—all the worlds throughout the ten directions are the real body. The practice of the Self, which is the universal truth, is zazen. In other words, zazen is proof of the real practice of the universe. When I practice zazen, I am embracing the universe.

Your personal action is the action of the whole universe. You alone act as the universe. That is the meaning of deep Zen practice.

. . .

Zazen is the liberation from the infinite past and the infinite future. This is a subjective fact. That is, you observe it introspectively, within yourself. If things look bleak, the sun and the moon—all of heaven and earth—are dark. If I am happy, even pickled radish seems to smile. If I'm angry, even the door and windowsill seem to be angry. That is the way we were from our roots.

. . .

When we are born, our universe is born too. When we die, we take everything of our universe with us.

Though people say, "Sawaki has very few desires," in fact that is not true. It's only that I persevere. If I give in to my deep desires, I will hurt the Buddha, so I simply endure, that's all. Because I have many desires, I understand the deep desires of others. It's stupid not to realize the depth of one's desires. That's why I don't try to deny the fact. My desires follow a curve. They can be intense. While I have these intense desires, they lead me to the Buddha Way. Therefore, the more intense the desire the better. When my desires wane, so does my energy. So my ability to resist grows when my desires increase. That's the importance of our lives coming together with the Buddha Way.

. . .

Every cell in the human body has the raw ingredients for worldly desires. So the problem is how we handle these desires. Though the flesh body is a burden, it is meaningless to squander it. Then you won't be able to practice zazen. You won't be able to rein in this burden in order to carefully handle it so that you have fulfilled your highest potential. Then you won't have converted these worldly desires into fine examples of bodhi, or wisdom. Though we all have various worldly desires, we can eliminate their burdens by the way we deal with them in our hearts.

. . .

Dealing with the Self without being sidetracked is the result of the supernatural powers of the gods.

Who are those who seek the truth? Deluded people? If they think like deluded people applying deluded thoughts, it would amount to nothing. On the other hand, do the so-called eminent people who work hard thinking they are creating something worthwhile really seek the truth? The Buddha Way does not come from the work we deluded people do. When we let go of our deluded work, the Buddha Way is there.

. . .

Because we view things through the eyes of the deluded, we can never understand zazen.

. . .

If you practice zazen, soon *you* will no longer be practicing. The great unbound will be practicing. That is the meaning of faith in zazen.

In zazen, you eliminate yourself and it is replaced by Mother Nature.

During zazen we meditate on the original storehouse of light within us and not on what will be. Since this is the way we have been from the beginning, we can become infants. There are those who think if they practice zazen they will become smarter or wiser, but that is not [true] zazen.

. . .

"If you practice zazen," many say, "you will become generous and be able to boldly express your feelings." That's ridiculous. Zazen is more like dancing on ice, like going through your life trembling about the dangers. That's what happens when you practice.

. . .

If you want to go from delusion to sainthood, you want the practice called *uiho* [Created things], not zazen. Zazen has no special instructions—just to sit is the mysterious art of our sect. That mysterious art of "just sitting" is the value of our practice.

Someone asked a practitioner of the *nembutsu* if he felt gratitude as a result of reciting the *nembutsu*. His response was "I feel nothing special." I too feel that way. Everyone makes a commotion about having a satori, or wanting to have a satori. I've passed my seventieth year now and it's still nothing special.

. . .

What's the purpose of my being born? You may put on the face of someone important, but in fact it is nothing special. There is nothing special for any of us. That is what we call no-gain.

. . .

No-gain is the most beautiful thing for a human being.

Though some people think that Zen practice is difficult, it is simply how we live our daily lives. Which means our attitude toward our lives. Dogen Zenji calls it the practicing Buddha. We make zazen our foundation and we practice our whole life with this body—that is the Buddha Way.

. . .

My faith is in zazen. I believe in the seated practice. "Dignified Bearing" is the Buddha Way—the ritual itself is the teaching of our sect. You must make this practice your object of worship. Without this practice, we have nothing we can call the object of worship. Our true object of worship is built upon our attitude toward life.

. . .

We see with our eyes, eat with our mouth, breathe with our nose; this is the great freedom. Delusion is losing sight of this true Self.

Stand on the high ground of the Buddha Way and don't cause havoc on the low ground. Which means to understand the Self that is all of heaven and earth, and return to your daily life without losing your presence of mind.

. . .

You don't attain satori from religious practice. Religious practice is itself the only satori.

. . .

Whether or not you've thought about it, zazen is being Buddha without any particular relationship to your thinking.

Without thinking of becoming a Buddha or thinking of anything, just sitting quietly is zazen. It is the perfect relaxation for humans.

. . .

Zazen is the way this five-*shaku* [approximately five-foot] body can live through eternity. It is the absolute living Dharma. If you ask what the highest form for a human birth is, it is for this five-foot body to be used by the great universe.

. . .

Zazen is a truly wondrous thing. It is not something you do after studying texts. It is in fact quite awesome.

To do zazen is proof of your having been given life from Mother Nature. It is not the regular self, but rather the continuation of the universe. In other words, the whole universe becomes you. It is the universe that reaches every nook and cranny—there is no place where it is not. So when one person does zazen, the whole universe is doing zazen. The universe is the content of the Self.

. . .

What we call zazen is practicing with all sentient beings. Just the practice alone brings into the human world an extraordinary religious drive.

. . .

What will you become if you practice zazen? You'll become all of heaven and earth. Truman, Mao, everyone is in my zazen.

With *shikantaza* there's not even enough room to add water.* That's why it requires a lot of energy. It's where the breath is. It's not practiced in order to become enlightened. It's not for anything. It's zazen with all one's might. It's "just sitting."

. . .

What we call the "faith-mind" is not our discriminating illusory mind. We are not fooled by the discriminating mind. To express it in words, it is believing in our true Self.

. . .

Zazen is the transparent Self. Nothing shows you yourself more than zazen. You can clearly see your unpleasant side. The purer the zazen, the more transparent it is. The more transparent it is, the more you can see your dirty self. To know the true Self, it's best to do zazen.

* It's complete in itself.

In zazen we don't hold on to our individual selves—it's the only time we can let go of our individuality. As long as we are able to let go of our individuality, we will become the whole universe. If we cannot do this and we hold on to our individuality, tending to this flesh body, wondering how much money one has, how much education, how long one is practicing zazen, it will all amount to nothing.

. . .

The true Self is not something that is within one's cognizance. We are cognizant of others with whom we compare ourselves. Just as we can't see our form when we are asleep, we can't see our true Self. Though we can't see or know our true Self, we can be it. I can be my true Self through zazen.

. . .

Do zazen and [eventually] it will rid you of the dregs of zazen.* It's important to remove the bitterness and harshness. You will feel natural. You will become sober. You will become sane.

* Pride, etc.

From the blank sheet of zazen everything will be seen.* You won't be seeing it yourself. It will be a Self alone delivered by zazen—a Self beyond words that you will feel in sync with.

. . .

Many people come to me and say, "When I do zazen distracting thoughts arise." You realize why you know distracting thoughts arise? It's because when you practice zazen you calm down and notice the distracting thoughts. Zazen is colorless and transparent. That's why those thoughts and ideas are so clearly evident.

. . .

In response to someone saying, "I do zazen but never reach a state of no-thought, no-form": You are making "no-thought, no-form" into something outside of yourself; that kind of zazen comes to nothing. It is after all a thought/idea, something other than you.

* Like a screen that shows numerous pictures.

Zazen is practicing Buddha in an ordinary person's body. It's not important that you become conscious of this. Thinking about what you will become [from zazen] has no value; it's nothing more than the karma of the ordinary person.

. . .

In zazen, you sit up straight, believing in this Way. That is the wonderful Dharma of *shikantaza* [just sitting].

. . .

Zazen is like entering your coffin—you do it whether you like it or not. So sit thinking you have died.

Humans hate tedium. "What can I do to avoid tedium? What can I do to entertain myself?" We spend our lives playing with toys. How wonderful tedium can be! Spend your life doing zazen—stretching time.

. . .

In our zazen sect, we do not sit preparing for satori. We just sit. When we practice zazen we truly need nothing—no pen, no notebook. We don't care about satori of delusion. We need to take nothing with us. We simply practice, as is, just doing it. This is too boundless, too simple, too flavorless for most humans. Humans can't understand what it's all about.

. . .

Do zazen and you are a practicing Buddha—very simple, easy to say. Then, before you know it, you stop practicing. That is profaning religious practice. Also, if you practice and become attached to it, your practice can become polluted. So if you don't become careless, and don't follow a self-centered tendency to follow the flow of a polluted practice, you will be "just sitting." At first it will not be easy. That is *shikantaza*.

Shikantaza is not something we do more or less. We have to understand it thoroughly. Though we say "just sit," we don't sit in a kind of fog. You have to put all your energy into sitting, aiming decisively.

. . .

Just practice zazen for itself. The aim of zazen is zazen—it is the other shore, the highest value. We don't do it to be a Buddha.

. . .

If you ask what zazen is, it is playing Buddha. So it is not work; it is play—playing Buddha.

Make the universe your concern. Make eternity your concern. Then you need bother yourself about nothing else. One who sits firmly with that resolve has an unmovable Buddha mind.

. . .

Shikan [from *shikantaza*] means "just" or "only that." I mean the "just" as in "just talking" or "just practicing zazen" or "just a potato." A life in which you are not led around by your paycheck, I call *shikan* or "just."

Third generation in the Kodo Sawaki line. At the Valley Zendo, from
left to right: Shohaku Okumura, Eishin Ikeda, and Koshi Ichida

From Kodo Sawaki's commentary on the Shodoka

The first volume of Sawaki's lectures of his twenty-one books with
Daihorin, publisher of his collected works, was his commentary on
the *Shodoka* (Song of Enlightenment), a poem attributed to Yoka
Genkaku Daishi, a disciple of the Sixth Patriarch of Zen.

Yoka spent one night with the Sixth Patriarch, Huineng, receiving his approval in that short time. Yoka had studied widely before
visiting Huineng and was already considered an advanced Buddhist

practitioner. He studied Tendai Buddhism and was said to have awakened after reading the Vimalakirti Sutra. Though both Huineng and Yoka considered their realizations as coming from within, it is interesting to note that they both had epiphanies from reading sutras (in Huineng's case it was the Diamond Sutra).

In the selection from the *Shodoka*, as with most of the excerpts throughout this book, Sawaki talks most about meditation. He divided his lectures on the poem into seventy-eight sections. The poem consists of 170 lines of seven Chinese characters each. This selection is from the forty-fourth section.

[Quotes from the text are in bold type]

We lose the Dharma treasure and destroy its merits
Because we rely on discriminating thoughts.
That's why Zen disciples reject this [thinking mind]
And through the power of wisdom immediately enter the unborn.

. . .

"Losing the Dharma treasure and destroying its merits" is a result of the mind that creates deluded thinking. With this mind we create happiness and misery. The misery we feel as a result of being poor is created by the mind many years after our birth. No baby feels sorry for itself for being born into poverty—feeling sorry for oneself comes much much later. When it is born, the baby has no feeling about being poor, whether or not a god exists, whether ghosts are real, whether there is a hell; all of these things come later and are driven by the thinking mind. They are delusions. Because of this deluded thinking, the foundation of Buddhism is compromised.

"That's why Zen disciples reject this thinking mind." This thinking mind means deluded thinking. Here we have plenty of water. To humans, water is water; to fish it is their dwelling place. We see things in accord with our karma at that time. When one is dying of thirst, a cup of tea feels irresistibly refreshing, but not when you have a headache. We see one thing in various ways, depending on how we are thinking and feeling about it. So what we call a fact may get totally lost. If we stop the thinking mind, the truth will be disclosed. It will be completely revealed. Quit driving the discriminating mind, quit measuring intellectual understanding, and avoid mental constructions; if all cease to exist, reality will manifest.

Daichi Zenji wrote, "The actualization of ultimate reality is beyond analytical reasoning," meaning the actualization of ultimate reality can't be calculated. It doesn't exist simply because we say it does, and it doesn't disappear just because we don't express it. Whether we express it or not, it neither increases nor decreases. It is the one unique reality.

So we practice zazen, and all discriminating thoughts—all thinking—solidifies. Because of this practice, these concepts are revealed and rejected; this one is swept away, that one is swept away; all are completely purged. They disappear, having been rejected as deluded thoughts of our ordinariness. The moon simply becomes the moon, the mountains are the mountains, and the sea is the sea. Heaven and earth have the same origin, all things are one, nothing is fabricated. This is the "Actualization of Ultimate

Reality." Through the power of seeing and knowing, one immediately enters the unborn.

Because in the unborn there is no birth, there consequently is no death. What we call "the samadhi of the unborn" is absolute. You enter this absolute through the power of seeing and knowing. That is the seeing and knowing Buddha. The seeing and knowing Buddha wipes out the minds of ordinary deluded people. This seeing and knowing Buddha, which opens the door to Buddha-wisdom, is the most important aspect of the Dharma. That's why it is written, "Zen disciples reject the thinking mind." In other words, you give yourself completely to zazen.

When I give myself completely to zazen, nothing any longer exists—there is no Sawaki. When there is no Sawaki, there is no deluded thinking mind. When this mind is rejected, nothing remains other than zazen. During zazen, one is in harmony with the Buddha, the Dharma, the founders, and the patriarchs. One becomes the entire universe. Through the power of the Knowing-Buddha, we enter into the unborn. This power resides in zazen. Through this knowing, illusions disappear and one immediately enters the unborn.

That's why Zen Master Keizan says at the beginning of his *Zazen Yojinki* [A Record of Points to Watch in Zazen]:*

"Zazen allows people to directly illumine the mind and reside comfortably in their fundamental nature. This is called reveal-

* Keizan Jokin (1268–1325) was the fourth patriarch of Soto Zen and founder of Sojiji Monastery.

ing one's original face and manifesting the scenery of one's true foundation." Again, "if you wish to illumine this mind, you must let go of all learning, throw away the Dharma of both the world and the Buddha, and set yourself apart from all delusion. When you actualize this unique true mind, the clouds of delusion will disappear and the true mind will be as clear as the bright moon.

"Zazen will then wipe out ignorance, and you will attain Buddhahood *as you are*. So you do not realize the unborn through the power of reasoning, but rather through the power of zazen."

Kodo Sawaki practicing zazen
(Photograph courtesy of Daihorin Publishers)

From a talk Sawaki gave on the Fukanzazengi (The Universal Recommendation of Zazen) in March 1936

People have many ideas about what Zen is. I'm often asked, "What is Zen?" My response is "to know the Self."

I am an advocate of Zen Master Dogen's teaching and have been for tens of years. I give talks about it and have been actualizing it in practice. This "knowing the Self" is beyond verbal explanation—it is beyond words and must be practiced. If I were to try to express this Self that is beyond words, I would have to say "the Self that selfs itself."*

Zen is wall gazing—you face a wall and you sit. You become yourself and only yourself. This Self that is only the Self is Buddha. So you become Buddha, the Tathagata; that is to say, you become yourself completely.† Originally, we are temporary [borrowed] selves—there is a screw on the outside—it's like a toy car that operates when the screw is turned. Only it's not a screw on the outside—it's the self operating the Self.

This is my zazen. I believe it is different from the usual concept of what the word zazen means. Satori is not essential, just be yourself. What do we have to do to become our selves? When we eat too much because the food is delicious, or when we refrain from eating because we don't like the flavor, that [attitude] is not coming from our [true] Self. We are being manipulated by something outside of us. Don't allow that to happen. What should we do to prevent that from happening? How can we act from our true Self? Do zazen. Practicing from the true Self is the meaning of zazen.

* I believe Sawaki is trying to describe the Self, which includes all. Shunryu Suzuki called it "big mind."
† In Pali it means thus-comes, thus-goes, thus-perfected one. It is one of the ten titles of the Buddha.

However, Dogen's Zen practice is quite simple. It is different from what people normally think of as established Zen practice. You have to go back to the teaching that existed before the arrival of the Sixth Patriarch [Huineng]. After the Sixth Patriarch, Zen developed a style that was flamboyant, making use of rough treatment and abusive language. It had changed from the pure, simple style of earlier times. What I refer to as Dogen's Zen is the pure teaching that existed before the appearance of the Sixth Patriarch.

In Dogen's *Bendowa* [Talks on the Wholehearted Practice of the Way] chapter of the *Shobogenzo*, he says, "It's a mistake to think of Zen as one of the three studies—precepts, meditation, and wisdom—or to think you can look at the Zen Way as one of the Six *Paramitas* [perfections]—generosity, ethical conduct, patience, effort, meditation, and wisdom or insight."

The name Zen school was derived by ordinary folk ignorant of the True Dharma Eye Treasury, the single great matter, the unsurpassable true Dharma. These folks called it the Zen sect and rejected it. It was this Zen that long ago was bestowed upon Mahakashapa alone by the Buddha at Vulture Peak, indicating the authentic transmission [of Zen].

This great Dharma Sermon on Vulture Peak was [witnessed by] five hundred direct disciples and many more, all excitedly waiting for the great event. At that time, the Buddha, to the amazement of the community, presented a flower without saying a word. Only Mahakashapa, the number one disciple, smiled. The Buddha said, "The unsurpassed teaching of the True Dharma Eye Treasury of the Wondrous Mind of Nirvana, I bestow on Mahakashapa," transmitting to him the Great Dharma.

This "holding up a flower and smiling faintly" way of communicating is equivalent to radio waves of the same wavelength. It's like switching on the radio and the waves merge. Now the Zen switch is turned on and the waves must match. As long as the waves are in sync, a two-thousand-year time interval or thousands of miles' separation, and still, I am Buddha and the Buddha is me. I am Bodhidharma and Bodhidharma is me.

That's the way Zen functions. It is what we call "mind-to-mind transmission"—like magic. It is the passing down [over the years] of the human essence, the path that functions naturally in humans *as they are.*

The beginning [of this transmission] was when the Buddha held out a flower and his disciple Mahakashapa smiled. This mind-to-mind transmission, this picking of the flower of the Buddha mind, is the transmission of the Great Way from teacher to disciple. It is called "Transmission of the Lamp." The flame of the teacher is imparted to the student. The teacher's flame is like a flame on a candle and is transferred to a torch. So even though the personalities are different, what I call the flame is only one; it is the same flame that is passed on. One candle is lit, someone lights a match with it, then a piece of wood is lit, and then a charcoal briquette. Whatever you light with the flame will be on fire when the Way is passed on. Whether it be a scholar, an unlearned person, a rich person, or a poor person, the Way of the past, present, or future is transmitted. It is after all Zen. So it is very different from the so-called [Buddhist] scholarship. It is different from what you can get from examinations. Because it directly touches a person's character, it is not something one ordinarily learns from another and it can't be memorized. It is not scholarship; it is one's life—it is something [already existing] within your character.

To put it in another form, this Way is transmitted as the subject of a person's character through his or her life. So how do we learn this? By practicing zazen.

In the *Bendowa* is written, "All Buddha-tathagatas transmit this wonderful teaching, actualizing the highest realization for which there is an unsurpassable means. This teaching, which has been transmitted directly from Buddha to Buddha, has the Samadhi of the Self as its principle." Which means, all the Buddhas are enlightened to the unsurpassable Way—which is zazen.

Since zazen is harmonizing wavelengths, we can't function in a contorted manner. We have to sit up straight.

I recommend to husbands and wives engaged in battle to put their hands in prayer position. You can't very well put your hands in that position and engage in fighting. Even if you say you want to fight, can you really do so while in that pose? Place your hands in prayer and do zazen and you are harmonizing with the wavelength of the Buddha. When you are harmonizing with the Buddha, you are no longer a deluded person.

If you wear a mask, hood, gloves, and rubber *tabi* socks and sneak into a person's house, you are a crook. Even if you were honest until the day before, you are still a crook. Even if you say, "This was my first heist, and I did it for only an hour," you can't expect that one hour of thievery to be considered small change compared to your previous thirty years of honesty. That won't do. On the other hand, if until now you were a gang member but now you start practicing zazen, you become a Buddha.

There is a subtle meaning in the form people adopt. Simply putting one's hands together in the proper position can make it difficult for husband and wife to argue. When an argument is about to begin, if the couple put their hands together in prayer, the heat of the moment when they readied themselves to fight will cool down.*

Look at our Zen form. Try to view it earnestly and learn from it. It is a truly outstanding form. With it you can change the direction [of your life]. This Way was not something invented by an idiot. It has been around since ancient times, so I am not referring to something that was created yesterday or today. This Way has been around for over a thousand, maybe ten thousand years. Zen monks often call it "the original nature." What is our original nature?

When we steal, that is not our original nature. When we overeat, that is not our original nature. If we are following our original nature, then our true way is not to overeat. Because we feel lowly, we fill our bellies until we can't store any more. That is not our original nature.

"The Way has existed since the beginning of the universe" was written as an opening statement to the Way in the *Fukanzazengi* [The Universal Recommendation of Zazen]. In other words, if you look into it, the Way is originally perfect, so why should we distinguish between practice and realization?† It also stated, "The

* Kodo Sawaki was never married!
† In a section that follows, Sawaki explains the Chinese ideograms from the text. I have skipped that section because it is confusing when translated into English.

vehicle of truth is naturally free, so why should we make an effort? The whole body is free of dust, so who would believe in a method to sweep it away? The Way is never separated from where you are, so what is the reason for training?"

This means that the Way was not created by man; it existed from the beginning. It's not a matter of wanting to practice or not; it has no relation to that. If you have a desire to make it greater, Buddha Dharma is not something that can be made greater, and neither is it something that can be made smaller because you want it to be such. The Buddha Dharma from the beginning is the whole heaven and earth.

That is why [Dogen says] "the Way is not separated from where you are." [Where you are] means the truth. Since it fills heaven and earth, who can shrink it or expand it? That is the origin of the Way. Though the Way is as stated, in the same *Fukanzazengi* is written, "However, if there is the slightest deviation, you will be as far from the Way as heaven is from earth."*

There is an error related to the statement from Mahayana Buddhism, "The mind itself is Buddha."† So, [the reasoning goes] if we are Buddha the way we are, then we can go to the Pure Land without chanting *Namu Amida Buddha*. If we can attain the Way without doing zazen, why would I bear the pain in my legs practicing? This is a mistaken view of Mahayana Buddhism.

When I went to give a talk in a country temple, a young priest asked if he could give an introductory talk before me.

---

* Compare this to the opening statement in the *Shinjinmei* (Believing in Mind).
† See the thirtieth case in the *Mumon kan* (The Gateless Gate).

"Go ahead," I said, and listened to his talk.

"The principle of Mahayana Buddhism is, this body *as it is* is Buddha. Since this body *as it is* is Buddha, there is no need for religious practice, and no need to worry about regressing; whatever you do is okay."

I thought that he was making a serious mistake.

After that I gave my talk. "If we leave things as they are, we become deluded people—when we eat, we overeat; when it's hot, [we complain] it's too hot; when it's cold [we complain] it's too cold; if you are rich or poor [you complain]. We are all hopelessly deluded, so we have to do something if we want to be Buddhas. We can't be Buddhas by doing nothing. So there is no meaning in saying 'this body is Buddha.'"* When I said this, contradicting the young priest, he was visibly disturbed.

That's why as I quoted the *Fukanzazengi* before: "However, if there is the slightest deviation, you will be as far from the Way as heaven is from earth. If even the slightest degree of disorder occurs, you will be lost in confusion."† For instance, you may feel proud of your understanding, or you may feel richly gifted with special powers of insight, attaining the Way, clarifying your mind . . . Such states, these "special powers of insight," are like lighting a match and having a satori and uncovering wisdom.

Next we have "Though they are only rambling around the

* Here Sawaki contradicts things he's said at other times, but he seems to be trying to impress upon his audience the need to do zazen.
† We find the same quote in the *Shinjinmei*.

border of the Way," which means they are entering and exiting the gates of satori, and then, "There is still a lack of action to let go of the body. What's more, the master of Jetavana Park, enlightened from birth, sat in zazen for six years. And [Bodhidharma] wall-gazed for nine years at Shaolin Temple."

The master of Jetavana Park is Shakamuni Buddha; and Bodhidharma, as you know, spent nine years facing a wall practicing zazen. Hence, next is written, "We should cease studying words and letters and withdraw to the light within, and study your own true nature now." So you can't say it's okay not to practice zazen. There is no way one can be enlightened without religious practice.

In Dogen's teaching we say, "Manner equals Buddha Dharma, and ritual is identified with the teaching." During the Tokugawa period [1600–1868], the Japanese people were pressured from the powers above: "You should obey, but never question why." We too were pressured with the words "Manner equals Buddha Dharma, and ritual is identified with the teaching" and scolded into showing the proper decorum.*

The manner referred to above is not the bowing to authority as we were taught during the Tokugawa period. The Buddhist manner is an attitude. That is an attitude expressed in the Buddhist teaching. When you adopt that attitude, the attitude of a Buddha, you become a Buddha. When you adopt the attitude of Bodhidharma, you become Bodhidharma. You are on the same

---

* By "we," I believe Sawaki is referring to monks during his training days.

wavelength as Bodhidharma. That is religious practice—you are a Buddha when you practice with the attitude of a Buddha.*

"I can practice spirituality [mentally], but when it comes to the body, I let it sleep." You suppose you can quickly wake up the spirit while you let the body sleep. Spiritually you cultivate the mind while you let the body live like a deluded person. The mind will try to drag the body along with it, but the body is too heavy to be pulled along, so only the mind will be taken care of. It's like a dream—like eating sweet cakes in a dream, but you will never be satisfied. I don't know about spirituality, but first you have to take good care of your body—that is the religious practice of Zen. Spirituality alone is the practice of a trickster.

There are novice monks who say, "Even when I play ping-pong, I am spiritually practicing zazen." Leave spirituality for now and carefully practice with your body. If you practice carefully with your body, you won't be in danger. At the beginning you won't understand spirituality. So we say, when your body is bent on one side or another we can easily correct it right there.

When we think about "Manner equals Buddha Dharma—ritual identified with teaching," we realize in Dogen's right Dharma there is quite a lot of instruction based on form [of the body].

So you need not concern yourself with enlightenment. Just try to keep the form, create a true Zen atmosphere, make a real Zen dojo [training center], eat good Zen food, develop an au-

* "If we are all endowed with Buddha Nature, we must act like Buddhas"—Shunryu Suzuki.

thentic Zen attitude, and foster a true feeling and life situation. That is, after all, the religious experience. When you act in accord with this religious experience, in other words when you practice it, and through this true practice it becomes a part of you—that is the Zen of Dogen. This is what is called *myoshu* [Excellent Training].*

What we refer to as satori [in our school] is not something we have to uncover now. As I said before, we already possess it, and have from way, way back. "The Way is originally perfect." That is "original enlightenment"—there is no beginning to enlightenment.

One often hears in Zen, "Approximately how many years do I have to practice?" It's as if one is an apprentice blacksmith asking how many years he would have to study before he can become a bona fide blacksmith, thinking about Zen in this manner. Zen is not like that. There is no end to religious practice.

There are Zen monks too who don't understand this. Some understand, but many don't. They feel there is something incomplete [in their practice]. "I can't take it," they complain. "No matter how much I practice, there is no point when I graduate." Well, it's the same with one's life. You don't graduate from your life. Zen practice is your whole life. That's the meaning of "original enlightenment." It's not like a play on stage, but more like the dressing room backstage. Of course there is *myoshu*, which occurs on stage. Original enlightenment is without differences. *Myoshu*

---

* *Myoshu* is a Soto Zen term for meditation based on the enlightenment of the Buddha.

makes distinctions. In the backstage everyone is equal, but on the stage distinctions are born.

Though many people call it "authentic Buddhism," the real nature of the unconditioned Dharma we call "original enlightenment." In the original state of the phenomena, there is no large or small. Hence there is no such thing as big Dharma.

However, since *myoshu* is on the stage, it can't be original enlightenment. There are actors backstage like Kono Moro Nao . . . [*Sawaki names a number of famous actors of that time*] who play men and women, likable and hateful, who get angry or treat others affectionately—roles that do not in fact exist [in original enlightenment]. They are like the design patterns of the backstage.*

. . .

In Akita Prefecture there was a Pure Land priest who lived many years ago. His name was Gakushin. A fellow once came to his place and said, "I can't recite the *nembustu,* so what should I do?"

Gekushin said, "An idle person like yourself will never recite the *nembutsu* until you really have no choice."

There was a song that pointed to this state of affairs:

---

* Sawaki is relating the actors on stage to discriminating knowledge. It changes according to circumstances. Backstage he likens to an unchanging reality, which he often calls the real Self. Compare his use of actors on stage with Advaita Vedanta teachers who equate the motion picture screen to the unchanging Atman and the projected pictures on the screen as the changing world.

If you don't shake it with your heart,
It won't clap.
Deep fog in the mountain field of Aki,
[Bird frightening] clapper.

If you don't shake it, it won't rattle.* All sentient beings possess the light of the Buddha Dharma, but if we don't practice, it won't amount to anything.

Here you have a match, and if you strike it a flame will appear. But if you don't know how to strike it, nothing will happen. The match is likened to *honsho*, original enlightenment. Striking it is likened to *myoshu*, excellent training. Learning how to strike the match is religious practice. You say you struck the match last year, so now you know that striking the match will create a light. You have the basic knowledge—that striking a match creates a light.

[Back to the example with the clappers,] religious practice is like shaking the clappers or striking a match. If you pull the rope to make the clappers sound in order to scare the birds away, do it once and it is not two. For the two to become one, you have to be active; under all conditions, you have to pull the body along.†

In other words, if you practice striking a match, the Dharma Nature or the Buddha Nature will emerge. The statement "There

---

* This refers to a rope with pieces of bamboo or wood hanging from it. When you shake it, it would rattle and scare birds from farmers' fields.

† I assume Sawaki is talking about eliminating dualism, i.e., two being dual.

is no end to Buddhist practice" refers to enlightenment. It's important for us humans to polish our own character.* In other words, the light will not appear unless we strike the match. We have to realize that there is no end to religious practice.†

---

* Here the word "polish" points to the famous koan where polishing a tile was equated to practice and Matsu was reprimanded for thinking that meditation (polishing) leads to becoming a Buddha. Most traditions see it as a condemnation of practice, but Dogen interprets it differently. For Dogen, practice and enlightenment are separate events, but both are essential.

† We have to assume that since Sawaki studied Dogen extensively, he understood Dogen's message that practice and enlightenment are two separate but essential components to Buddhism. Sawaki is talking to people of many traditions and to many laypersons. So he may not have wanted to go into the subtleties of Dogen's understanding that practice is necessary but is not something that leads to enlightenment.

The following is a 1952 interview with Kodo Sawaki for NHK (Japanese Public Radio). The announcer, whose name was left out of the transcript, is asking the questions.

. . .

ANNOUNCER. Sensei, you were wounded during the Russo-Japanese War. Where was the battle?

SAWAKI. It was the thirty-seventh year of Meiji [1904]. We were passing through Shusambo [Cairn Hill Fortress].

ANNOUNCER. Shusambo? That would be Tachibana's battalion?

SAWAKI. Yes, Tachibana and the regimental commander, Sekiguchi. There was a heavy battle at dawn, a particularly fierce battle—complete destruction.* We lined up to give support to the regulars. That afternoon about three o'clock a bullet hit me and I collapsed.

ANNOUNCER. Were you in the reserves?

SAWAKI. No, I wasn't. I was drafted—we supported the main group.

ANNOUNCER. Were monks included [in the draft] at that time?

SAWAKI. Yes, they were. Only in America were pastors exempt. In Japan they didn't believe in [religious exemption]. We were all eligible for the draft.

ANNOUNCER. Then you were special forces, as a rear guard?

---

* Sawaki doesn't say which side was destroyed.

SAWAKI. Yes, you see, Buddhism was on the decline. The country wasn't supporting religions. The international situation was also part of the reason.

ANNOUNCER. And it must have been difficult for you to give talks because of your mouth.*

SAWAKI. Yes, I couldn't speak for six months after I was wounded. It was difficult. The doctor said as I got used to my condition I would be like a baby trying to sound out words—if I made a concentrated effort, he said, I would be able to talk again. When I began to talk again the wound made it very painful, because it split my tongue. I couldn't pronounce the ends of words. But as the soreness decreased, I was able, with great effort, to say most words.

ANNOUNCER. Sensei, did you come from a Buddhist home?

SAWAKI. No, my family wasn't Buddhist or any other religion.

ANNOUNCER. Really. Then how did you make the connection with Buddhism?

SAWAKI. Well, my parents both died when I was young. I didn't become a monk because of their death, but I did begin to brood over the meaning of life, wondering why I had to spend my life like this.

My house was in a red-light district.† I was raised in a back-alley slum. We were very poor when my parents died. I was adopted in an area where there were many different types of people,

---

* Sawaki had been shot through the neck during the Russo-Japanese War and the bullet split his tongue.
† Sawaki jumped to describing his adoptive family's home.

and I saw how people lived on a trivial stage. So I would sneak out from my adoptive parents' house and go to temples.

At that time I was learning wherever I went. I saw some pretty unsavory characters and lifestyles. When I was twelve or thirteen, I battled within myself over that.

ANNOUNCER. I see. And you say you were [only] twelve or thirteen at the time?

SAWAKI. Yes. On the one hand I listened to some beautiful talks, while on the other hand were these unsavory things. You see, as a child I was made to stand lookout for my [adoptive parents'] gambling house. That being as it was, I lived and experienced that world firsthand. I guess that's why I reacted by longing for the opposite—searching for a clean world. I was living in Ishinden near Ise. Ishinden housed the main temple for the Takada sect of Pure Land Buddhism. Pure Land Buddhism flourished there, so I often visited temples there and felt gratitude for Amida Buddha.

ANNOUNCER. So you went there on your own?

SAWAKI. Yes, from my childhood I had somehow felt that I understood. That was my motivation then, to throw away my life for the sake of the Way. Then something I heard, an extremely important thing [for me] about a boy throwing away his life for the sake of the Way. It was from the Nirvana Sutra. The boy, Sessen Doji, in search of the Way, was willing to give up his life. While searching for the Way, he didn't hesitate to throw away his life. Well, I heard this wonderful story. Soon after that I ran away from home thinking I too should be willing to throw away my life for the sake of the Way.

I received two *sho* of rice and set out for Eiheiji Monastery in Echizen.* From Ise it is approximately seventy *ri*.† I walked the whole way. I stood in front of the monastery gate and said, "I want to be a monk." A monk met me at the gate and said, "You can't become a monk here." Since they wouldn't let me in, I said, "I can't think about anything other than becoming a monk, so let me die here." The monk responded, "No, I can't let you die here, it would cause problems."

ANNOUNCER. How old were you then?

SAWAKI. Seventeen.

ANNOUNCER. Seventeen?

SAWAKI. For two days and nights I stayed there until another monk came out and said, "Follow me." He took me in and fed me rice gruel. That was the beginning, but I didn't stay at Eiheiji very long. Even now I've continued this [traveling] throughout my life.

ANNOUNCER. In that way, your strong mind led you to the gate of the Buddha. After that, how shall I say it, did you have other problems?

SAWAKI. I'm human after all, so I had many problems.

ANNOUNCER. What about once you entered the Buddha Way?

SAWAKI. Right . . . Before that, things were different. When I entered Eiheiji there was no heaven and no satori. I was just a human being with no learning, so it wasn't easy.

I just had to figure out what to do—that was one concern. I

---

* One *sho* is approximately eight cups.

† One *ri* is approximately four kilometers.

thought that it would help if I read books, but they only increased my knowledge and did nothing for my body. That's the way humans operate; we are strange [*laughs*].

ANNOUNCER. Normally, when someone enters the monastic way, after years of training he takes charge of a temple. That is the way we think of the usual course. In your case, Sensei, you have never taken charge of a temple. Is there some specific reason you chose this course?

SAWAKI. Well, in the beginning I did think I would take over a temple. Whether it was my fortune or misfortune I can't say. When I was about to do so, I saw these harsh legal battles over taking charge of temples. For me, [seeing that] was something for which I am grateful.

Monks go to court each claiming they're right—brother disciples. There was even a case where the younger brother disciple pulled his elder brother disciple down and became the head priest of the temple.

As a practitioner, if you're not powerful you will fall from grace.

This is foolishness. The real purpose for becoming a monk will have lost its meaning. All you will have is the possession of a temple. It may be a strange reason for me not wanting a temple, [*laughs*] but it's my life.

ANNOUNCER. If all monks thought like that, not taking charge of temples, it would be difficult for ordinary people.

SAWAKI. Ordinary people wouldn't be troubled.

ANNOUNCER. Really?

SAWAKI. Not having a temple, contrary to what you may

think, I feel is a good thing. Why do you think people take charge of temples? They say, "If we have a temple, we can make a living." It comes from that way of thinking. Well, that is a deluded way of thinking. It's okay not to make a living, isn't it? Didn't the Buddha throw away his princely life?

You have a temple and you feel like you are in the spiritual world. That's why there are so many legal battles—all these "prestigious" temples. I despise that [idea].

ANNOUNCER. Regarding so-called zazen, names like "wild fox Zen" are often talked about.* The person preaching this teaching may understand [what he preaches], but those around him may not. Sensei, what are your feelings about this?

SAWAKI. Of course, it is not the fault of what we think of as Zen. However, the one who says he is enlightened—calling himself enlightened, that is unfortunate. That person is most likely deluded. He is making a great mistake.

My idea of zazen is not something that you practice for years and pile up human knowledge and call it satori or zazen. It's not entering the perfect world, nor is it something we enter in one [big flash]. In other words, for me practicing zazen is establishing the best posture for a human being—a divine posture. So just to sit is all you need to do, just to sit and believe in it.

It is the same with regard to the *nembutsu*. You repeat the

---

* *Yako Zen*, or wild fox Zen, refers to people who without practicing zazen pretend to be enlightened and deceive others. I'm not certain that the announcer understood the above definition of wild fox Zen.

name, Amida Buddha. What does the name become? You believe the chant, and when you recite it, when the person recites it, he is immediately in heaven [the Pure Land].

In our zazen, as long as we sit, we are being Buddha. That is satori. In that respect, it is quite different than other approaches to zazen.

ANNOUNCER. Is it "no-thought, no-form"?

SAWAKI. No, I don't think of it as "no-thought, no-form," since we simply sit . . . in zazen.

ANNOUNCER. Is it something before "no-thought, no-form?"

SAWAKI. [True,] "no-thought, no-form" does not mean you sit in a kind of fog of no thought, no form—it's not like that. That's not what happens. It is simply being sane.

ANNOUNCER. So, contrary to that [what is thought of as no-thought, no-form], the most important thing to keep in mind is whatever you think is fine—whatever appearance you take is okay.

SAWAKI. Right . . . Appearance . . . As long as you sit with all your might.

It's the same with reciting the nembutsu; you can't recite it with no thought, no form. That's not possible, is it? That's silly . . . *Namu Amida Buddha, Namu Amida Buddha* [Praise to Amida Buddha]. That too means we are all born in the Pure Land *the way we are*. It's like that.

Also, it is written in the Lotus Sutra: "One praise to Buddha and all become Buddhas." That is the fundamental principle.

It's just like my example: become a robber, steal from peo-

ple, and you will immediately be a disciple of Ishikawa Goemon.*
Robbers are following the way of Ishikawa Goemon; zazen practitioners are following the way of the Buddha.

ANNOUNCER. While it's a little vague, I think I understand
what you are saying.

SAWAKI. The Buddha Way is actual practice. So at once your
life merges with the Buddha's life. He was a human being, thinking as humans do, and it can't be understood from the perspective
of techniques. That alone is the special feature of my zazen. That
is what Zen Master Dogen transmitted. It is the original mind of
Bodhidharma.

From the end of the Song Dynasty to the Yuan [and] Ming
dynasties techniques developed, and solving koans was the way
monks became respected for having had satoris. Well, today
[monks] have satoris, which in certain religious sects allows the
monks to be candidates to be head priests of temples.

That's the way they think. But they're wrong. Believe in zazen
itself, and if you put your whole body into it, that is [true] zazen.

* Ishikawa Goemon was an infamous robber who was caught and boiled in a
bathtub. Since then, that kind of tub is referred to as a Goemon Tub.

Kodo Sawaki on a return trip to his hometown, Ishinden.
The boy holding Sawaki's hand is Chikashi Hiramatsu,
son of the postmaster of Ishinden.

Introduction to "Scolded by Zen Master Dogen"

Kodo Sawaki was a charismatic Zen Master whose popularity was unmatched during the twentieth century in Japan. Like Zen Master Bankei (1622–1693) who attracted hordes of people to his talks, Sawaki's Dharma talks were spontaneous and sprinkled with personal anecdotes, which allowed his listeners to feel connected to both his ordinariness and wisdom.

"I am the most deluded person in the world" is an often-quoted saying of Sawaki. And he would add, "That is why I must practice zazen." He saw Zen meditation as a practice that watched over him and not as something one does in order to become enlightened. Sawaki's zazen was very much like the Vow of Amida Buddha. My friend, the monk Joko Shibata, called it "faith zazen."

It is not surprising that Sawaki's Zen has a strong True Pure Land Buddhist element to it. As he brings out in this talk, Saikichi Sawaki, the boy who would be ordained as Kodo, grew up in a town that was formed around the head Pure Land temple Senjuji, surrounded by its many branch temples. He attended many Pure Land sermons before he ran away to Eiheiji at seventeen years old. Though Kodo Sawaki spent most of his life interpreting the writings of Zen Master Dogen, there is, implicit in his interpretation, an understanding that one is already saved, and that the practice of zazen is not to give us something new, but rather to keep us aware of our inherent Buddha-nature.

Scolded by Zen Master Dogen
A lecture delivered by Kodo Sawaki in the twenty-eighth year of
Showa (1953)

What is religious practice? The common response is often that
it is some sort of backbreaking activity. However, our founder's
[Dogen's] teaching is based on our present [immediate] life and
nothing more. And that practice is zazen [Zen meditation]. We
meditate in accord with the Dharma, we eat in accord with the
Dharma, and we prepare food in accord with the Dharma. We
resolve, from the time we awake in the morning, as the ancient
saying goes, "to be conscious of everything, disregarding nothing in the ten directions." Our determination is constant from
the time we open our eyes. Examples of this teaching are written in Zen Master Dogen's *Shobogenzo* in the "Senmen" [Wash-
ing Your Face] chapter and "Senjo" [Washing and Cleaning]
chapter.

There is an ancient saying regarding bathing and going to
bed: "Take a breather from all activities and purify your heart/
mind and you won't be corrupted." In regard to that, in Dogen's
Bendoho [Rules for Practicing the Way], "If the community of
monks is sitting [in meditation], you should follow suit and sit;
if they are reclining, you should recline. Do as the community
does in action and in stillness. Don't part from [the activities of]
the monastery in death or life." I'd had many experiences in my
life, but the following phrase really astonished me: "There is no
advantage to being exceptional."

I'd always tried to outdo others, being extremely competitive in my youth. So when I read the *Bendoho,* I found myself banging up against this phrase. It was one of the major surprises in my life. That was followed by "We should not behave differently than the community [of monks]. That is the flesh and bones of the Buddhas and patriarchs. It is also our dropping off of mind and body—the practice/enlightenment [of our original state] in the beginning-less past—unrelated to manifestation. It is the koan before the existence [of phenomena]. Don't wait for a great satori."

For someone like me who had found his way into the community of Eiheiji Monastery, the [Buddhist] practice or experience was abstract and not at all a part of my core. As a child I had come to the realization that there was something more important than money and position. I would like to talk about that realization.

As most of you know, I was born into poverty, lost my parents, and was adopted. Next door to my adoptive parents was a poor backstreet store, the home of a sagely family—all extremely fine people and well educated. They traced their ancestry to a family of landlords and local magistrates. Circumstances affecting these people during the time of their parents' generation impoverished the family, and the father opened a scroll mounting and framing store. They had one child. When I was adopted, that boy was fifteen years old and I was nine.

My adoptive parents were gangsters operating a gambling house and didn't want me to be involved with such evil doings.

They wanted me to be respectable, so they introduced me to my educated neighbors.*

From then on, I often visited those people. It really felt good being around them. I stopped hanging out with other kids [my age] and went to my neighbors' house [instead]. The conversations I heard at their home stayed with me for the rest of my life.

The son from that family didn't go to middle school, high school, or college as boys from educated families today do. He studied the Analects of Confucius and Mencius and works from the Nine Chinese Classics at a private night school. I stuck by his side like a saddlebag, hanging out with him constantly. When he went to his night school class, I would walk with him part of the way and meet him on his way home. He would talk to me about Confucius, the Analects, Mencius, Raiki, and Monzen.† It was a truly joyful time.

From the time he was a child he was skilled at painting and wanted to be an artist. At seventeen or eighteen he decided to [formally] study painting. He apprenticed under a priest of the Pure Land sect in Kuwana City on the Ise Peninsula. The priest's name was Yuinen Hoyama. Besides learning about the Confucian classics, he told me many stories about artists. One story was

* Sawaki tells this story very differently elsewhere. He said he would have to pretend he was going to the public bath and sneak off to his neighbors' house. See Tanaka Tadao, *Sawaki Kodo – Kono Koshin no Hito* 沢木興道この古心の人 (Tokyo: Daihorin-kaku, 1995), 60.

† Raiki: The Book of Rites, from the Confucian canon. Monzen: A sixth-century Chinese collection of various writings.

about his teacher and about valuing something more than money or position.

Artists at the time of Yuinen Hoyama didn't charge [their clients] in advance for materials and didn't make deals with curiosity shop owners, raising prices for their work as they do today. Hence many artists were poor.

When Yuinen Hoyama was a child, he went to Kyoto to study painting. He went with the intention of studying with the artist Ikkei Ukita. Ukita Sensei was of the next generation to great artists like Okyo, Buncho, and Taigado. Hoyama arrived at the teacher's house and saw a plaque in front of a longhouse [a series of tenement houses all under the same roof] with Ukita's name on it.

This must be the place, he realized. He entered the complex and found Ukita's dwelling at the end of the longhouse.* It was raining and a shoemaker was fixing the teacher's shoes on the veranda. Ukita was sitting, talking with him.

When the young Hoyama entered the house, he noticed there was hardly enough room for a kitchen and studio. A nobleman sat at the far end of the narrow studio. The teacher would converse with the shoemaker and the nobleman, spending equal time with both men.

I heard this story and my child mind found it delightful. It was the twenty-something year of Meiji [1890s], still some time before the Sino-Japanese War, and Japan hadn't really changed

---

* Probably the least desirable spot of the dwellings of the longhouse. It is where the communal latrines and water pump usually are.

internally from the feudalism of the Tokugawa period. The nobleman and shoemaker were spoken to and treated as equals. I felt at
the time that humans must arrive at this level. Now talk of equal
treatment is not surprising, but back then treating a shoemaker
and a nobleman as equals was exciting to me.* I wanted to live my
life with that kind of sensibility.

There was another story my friend told me about Ukita Sensei. Once Ukita was asked to paint a figure of Kuan-yu.† He was
a warrior from the Three Kingdoms, brandishing a *seiryuu* sword
[a large, curved sword formerly used in China] and wearing a long
beard. Paintings of Kuan-yu were supposed to be splendid portraits and therefore required a lot of paint. They also required gold
leaf for glitter, copper rust green, and deep Prussian blue paint, all
very expensive. When Ukita finished the painting, it was a splendid portrait. Because he used so many expensive paints, Hoyama
assumed his teacher would surely charge a lot of money for the
painting. When he asked his teacher how much he charged for
the painting, Ukita said nonchalantly, "Oh that. I got two *bu*."
Two *bu* was equivalent to fifty *sen*.‡ Even with inflation, fifty *sen*
would not be enough to buy the paints. Hoyama was shocked. He
realized that no matter the cost, artists do the work even if they

---

* Shoemakers were outcasts in old Japan because they worked with leather (the
hides of animals were considered unclean).
† A Chinese warrior who was canonized in popular Chinese religion as
Kuan-ti, the god of war.
‡ This talk was given in 1953. A *sen* is 1/100 of a *yen*, and at the time 360 *yen*
was equal to a U.S. dollar.

lose money. And that was why he lived in a hovel at the end of a longhouse, a dwelling that leaned to one side.

Hoyama took five gold pieces, placed them in an envelope, wrapped it properly, and fabricated the story to his teacher that someone had asked him to give the money to Ukita and requested the artist paint him a landscape in return.

"Fine," responded Ukita.

Since Ukita had painted the Kuan-yu for two *bu*, five gold pieces was quite a sum. His teacher could use as much expensive paint as he pleased. Hoyama thought about the painting his teacher would create, secretly holding high expectations of the result. However, Ukita stretched the silk on the frame, rubbed a charcoal ink stick, dipped the brush in the tray of ink, and quickly brushed the landscape. Then with another brush, he added some light and shade, and gave Hoyama his five-gold-piece *sumie* painting. That's when Hoyama realized his teacher painted what his mood dictated. That's the story my friend told me.

Ukita talked with a nobleman and shoemaker as equals. He painted what his spirit ordained regardless of whether he was compensated with two *bu* or five gold pieces. The story truly delighted me. It made me want to become an artist. After that I studied painting with my next-door neighbor.

I lacked dexterity and would copy pictures from books or trace paintings with my unsteady hand. In the end I realized I didn't have the basic temperament. Even in my writing classes, I barely received passing grades and never went beyond elementary school. It was a hopeless situation. The same applied to my attempt at drawing. I tried to paint because I envied my next-door neighbor, but it was useless. Though I fixed lanterns at that time and painted until I was fifteen or sixteen, in the end I was simply no good at it.

I started making rounds to temples from the time I was thirteen or fourteen. From my childhood I lived in Ishinden, a town on the Ise Peninsula—the home of Senjuji, the main temple of the Pure Land Takada sect. There were about twenty to thirty branch temples all lined up in the area and others a few kilometers away. When there was a sermon in one of the temples, people would invite me and I would go along with them. I didn't go as a believer, but I recited the *nembutsu* with the others in the congregation and listened with them to the sermons.

When I was around seventeen, I came to feel uneasy about my life. I had no idea what I was supposed to do with my future. Once I started earning money, my adoptive parents just played around instead of working. They depended on me to work and to give them money. They discussed my future: "He's strong, works hard, and has a good physique," and, "When he reaches nineteen, we'll have him take a wife. Then we can retire."

This is terrible, I thought, my greatest fear. I struggled to earn this much money, drove myself hard so far, and now they want me to marry on top of that and have children. How difficult it would be to support a wife and children and care for my parents, too! This was the first major shock of my life.

On one hand I was taught about Confucius and Mencius, and on the other I was chanting to Amida Buddha, and now my parents tell me I'm going to support them in their retirement [which meant in their drinking and gambling]. This was quite a burden. I would then have to do something with my life. I'd need money to support my family. Wasn't that why so many Europeans went to America in hopes of making money? For Japanese at that time, going to work in Osaka was the common-sense thing to do.

Though I knew my parents wouldn't approve of me going to Osaka, at that time they were still healthy. If I left them to their own means and didn't take care of them, they certainly would be able to feed themselves. So while they were still healthy enough to take care of themselves, I would go to Osaka and make a lot of money. I'd work for a while, and when I'd saved enough to open a street stall I would do so and earn a living. Osaka was not that far. With fifteen *sen* and cold leftover rice taken from our last meal, I ran away to Osaka.

This plan turned out to be a big mistake. Osaka was too close. In those days, there was no Kansai train, so I had to take a roundabout way through Kyoto—a train went from Kyoto to Osaka. But eventually a relative came to get me. I'd met an old friend in Osaka who, out of kindness, sent a telegram to my folks, and as a result I was led back home.

My parents didn't yell at me. They were grateful to have me back. They had apparently made my relatives promise not to reprimand me. From then on, things returned to the way they were before I'd run away, and my parents' thinking remained the same.

I was troubled over what to do next. I finally decided to become a monk. At least that was the basis of my thinking. But I knew that if I took that step halfway, I might once again get caught. As I was considering how to go about this, I attended a

Buddhist sermon. It happened to be the story of Sessen Doji, a boy who'd secluded himself in the mountains to seek the Way. He heard a loud voice: "All things change / This is the law of life and death." According to folklore, the national teacher Kobo [Kukai] translated it as "The flowers, however fragrantly bloom, are doomed to wither. Who in this world can hope to live forever."*

"All things change / This is the law" is a serious warning. But to Sessen, this still didn't resolve things. There must be another verse. He wondered where the voice of the person who recited these verses came from. He looked around and saw a great big demon in front of him. Sessen asked, "Did you recite, 'All things change / This is the law of life and death'?" "Indeed, I did," responded the demon. "Please instruct me on the verses that follow. I came here in search of the Way, and I must know the verses that follow."

The demon responded, "I am hungry and can't say any more."

"Then, what do you eat?"

"I eat the warm flesh and blood of humans."

"I will give you my flesh and blood," Sessen said. "Just endure a bit longer and recite the next verses."

At that the demon recited, "Put an end to life and death / The bliss of nirvana is realized."

Then Sessen bit his finger and wrote the verses in blood on white rocks and the bark of trees. This was called the "vow of trees

---

* The quote attributed to Kukai continues and uses all the Japanese syllables in the form of a poem. The only connection to the story is that both indicate that life is impermanent. It says nothing about Nirvana.

and rocks." He was prepared to throw away his life in his search for the Way. After making this vow, he jumped from a tree into the demon's mouth.

However, the demon was really the Buddha in disguise, and his mouth became a lotus flower. The Buddha was moved by Sessen's desire to seek the Way. He then turned toward the heavens and left.

This was the sermon I heard.

Had I heard it today, or had I read it in the Nirvana Sutra, I might not have been that moved. But back then, hearing that verse, hearing about cause and effect, I was deeply moved. It was to guide me throughout my life.

That's right, I thought, I should stake my life on this. Fine, even if I don't succeed in becoming a monk, if I die truly attempting to become one, wouldn't that be the same? If I take half-hearted steps, I would never be able to become a monk or realize the Buddha Way and attain peace of mind.

So I resolved to run away from home. I had no idea where I should go, and only knew Pure Land Buddhist priests. So I visited one.

"Go to Eiheiji Monastery," the priest recommended. "Eiheiji is in Echizen, where people put aside their spades and hoes and bow when they see a monk. More importantly, I had the occasion to go to Eiheiji and traveled around attending various sermons. I was on a pilgrimage. It was a quiet place deep in the mountains, a place resembling the Pure Land."

Hearing that, I wanted to go there even if on the way I might die on the side of the road. The priest didn't suggest I become a

Pure Land monk, and his reason was strange. "If you become a Shin [i.e., Pure Land] monk, you'll be expected to take a wife. What would it mean to have a wife? Look at me. I have children and my wife is dead. Now I have three kids that piss in bed. I spend every night dealing with them. I'm presently in babysitting hell. Zen monks aren't expected to take wives. I'm not talking about whether you are allowed to have a wife. I'm saying it's okay not to have one. So become a Zen monk and don't take a wife. Then you can spread the faith as you wish and practice Buddhism freely."

So I headed for Eiheiji with two *sho* of rice, two candles, one book of matches, and two portions of cold medicine.* It took five days and nights, and when I arrived, I asked to be allowed to die there.†

"You can't die here," I was told. "Go somewhere else."

"I can't move," I said. "I'm famished."

Finally, a monk in laborer's clothes let me in and I became a monk.‡

However, difficulty followed me. It is not easy to find the right teacher, nor was it easy to find a true fellow Way-seeker. So I traveled to Kyushu without any money and spent two years practicing

---

* A *sho* is 0.48 U.S. gallons.

† Here Sawaki has jumped to having arrived at Eiheiji and being asked to leave. He said he couldn't move so they should let him die there.

‡ Here is another big jump. In another talk, Sawaki told how the head of labor took him in when he realized the young Sawaki wasn't about to leave, and fed him and allowed him to work as a laborer, which led to his eventually receiving robes.

in Amakusa [in Kumamoto Prefecture] and then in Tamba [in Hyogo Prefecture]. I was able to practice the Way though good teachers and good Dharma friends were rare. In fact, it was a most trying time for me, having become a monk and disregarding my parents' needs. I thought I would be better off dead, but here I was alive, so what could I do?

Then when I turned twenty, after many twists and turns in my life I arrived at Ryoun Fueoka's temple, Hosenji, in Yotsuji, Tango [in Kyoto Prefecture]. Fueoka Roshi spent a long time studying under Zen Master Nishiari. He was a peaceful, well-rounded teacher with a penetrating mind. His voice was beautiful and rare as a silver bell. He had a fragile body and was not that well known but was an extraordinary man. I practiced at his place, feeling it would be okay to be there for the rest of my life.*

At this fragile Abbot Fueoka's place, I first learned the way of life and practice of the descendants of Zen Master Dogen. Fueoka was soon transferred to Kakegawa City in Enshu [present-day Shizuoka] and I went with him. But shortly after, I was called to report for my physical examination for conscription. That was November of my twenty-first year. I had to report to the draft board in Nagoya on the first of December.

That period until the end of the Russo-Japanese War was

---

* For detailed and amusing stories about Sawaki's encounters with Fueoka, see Sakai, *Sawaki Kodo Kikigaki*. For English, see *Dharma Brothers: Kodo and Tokujoo*, 154–64.

like a blank period in my life. When the war was over, I resumed my studies. I also had to take care of my parents. I went to Horyuji Monastery and the Nara School of Buddhist Studies. At that time, the high priest Saeki of Horyuji was around forty years old and I was in my late twenties. I was taken under his wing for seven or eight years. Saeki was a highly reputed Buddhist teacher.

I may look at things differently than others. People selfishly guard the teachings—what they write and the books they own. I was deeply troubled by this attitude. I didn't pay the required monthly tuition and had nothing to give. I simply received. Saeki pampered me, watching over me, rambunctious as I was. If I have become open, it is a result of observing this high priest.

Saeki had an open door. He lent me books no matter how special they were to him. He took me by the hand, showing me his rare book collection, and even lent me books from it. This was a particular quality of Saeki not often seen in teachers.*

I studied *Yuishiki* [Consciousness Only], *Kusha* [Abidharma], and *Inmyoo* [Indian logic] with Saeki. When I was at Horyuji, there were lectures in Zen on the *Shobogenzo* at Sotan Oka Roshi's place, and *genzo* meetings at Eiheiji, which I attended. Oka Roshi stood unrivaled in his eye for the teachings.

At the first *genzo* meeting held at Eiheiji, Zen Master

---

* Sawaki printed copies of the teaching he used for his lectures with his own money and distributed them to his audience for free.

Nishiari was in his eighties and Oka Roshi was in his forties. Oka was asked to teach on behalf of Nishiari. He didn't simply take each phrase from the *Shobogenzo* and present it. He truly possessed a discerning eye—an extraordinary man. Oka Roshi was nominally the abbot of Daijiji Monastery in Kawajiri, Higo [present-day Kumamoto Prefecture]. Roshi sent me to be in charge of training the monks at Daijiji. I had to leave there after Oka Roshi died.

I have never been misguided by Dogen's teaching. To this day I have followed the practice of *shikantaza* without fail thanks to studying under Fueoka Roshi and under the discerning eye of Sotan Oka Roshi. For that I am truly grateful. And before that, as a child I'd heard stories from my neighbor about the artist Ikkei Ukita, who valued something far more than money or position.

So here I am today coming from that background. However, I'm now past seventy years old, a tame monk, no longer possessing the strong emotions of my impassioned youth. Abstractions like enlightenment and religious practice feel to me like an embarrassment.

When I was Saikichi the lantern maker, I realized there was something more valuable than money or position. So at seventeen I ran away from home and became a monk, and have been constantly scolded by Zen Master Dogen. I somehow managed to arrive at this place in my life. Now I'm a feebleminded old man, shuffling through life in this present condition.

Kodo Sawaki practicing zazen at Antaiji Temple in his final year

. . .

The following interview took place at Antaiji Temple in March 1965.
Kodo Sawaki was eighty-four at the time. He died on December 21 of
the same year. The interview was conducted by Shunpei Ueyama, associate professor of natural sciences at Kyoto University. Kodo Sawaki
had retired to Antaiji when his legs could no longer carry him.

UEYAMA. How long have you been here at Antaiji?

SAWAKI. I've been coming here every month for the past sixteen years.

UEYAMA. This temple has no affiliation, does it?

SAWAKI. Yes, it does. It's a Soto sect temple.

UEYAMA. Soto sect?

SAWAKI. Yes, it began as a temple for students [at Komazawa University] to do research. So it's not the usual temple—not a normal temple, it doesn't have a parish.

[Sokuo] Eto was the president of Komazawa University and became the abbot of Antaiji in name only. He had little to do with the running of the temple. When he died, he left me in charge—I had no choice. Before I came here, it was a ghost temple.

UEYAMA. You mean like a haunted house?

SAWAKI. During the war, homeless refugees stayed here. It became a house full of ghosts. There were sick people in this room and that one over there, and people who had died of tuberculosis during the war. There were many things . . .

UEYAMA. Roshi, you were very busy according to the books I read about you, until recently—until you entered here. When you moved into Antaiji, your life became quiet, didn't it?

SAWAKI. That's right.

UEYAMA. What is your daily life like?

SAWAKI. Strange, but I've never gotten bored.

UEYAMA. What do you do?

SAWAKI. I read books every day.

UEYAMA. Which books have you been reading?

SAWAKI. Many different kinds of books. Up until now I only read books I felt responsible to read, though some were interesting.* Now I read popular books about native peoples—some are written by Germans and some by Japanese. I read both.

* I assume he means Buddhist books.

UEYAMA. Which Japanese books do you read?

SAWAKI. The ones written by Japanese are very interesting. Today's science writers I find very good [*laughs*]. It's no good to be so freewheeling.

UEYAMA. Roshi, when did you begin your Zen practice?

SAWAKI. I got involved quite early. I went to Eiheiji Monastery to become a monk, at the beginning.

UEYAMA. At the beginning?

SAWAKI. Yes, I was repairing lanterns when I ran away from home and went to Eiheiji. At Eiheiji they practiced zazen according to Zen prescription, but their bodies and souls weren't really in it. They didn't want to practice, so they did it reluctantly.

Then there was this [affiliated] temple, Ryuunji, in the village of Hongo in a town that today would be Awara. We went to help out there for Obon.* When Obon was over and the cleanup and *segaki* were completed, all the helpers from Eiheiji [inaudible] somewhere, we were free to do whatever.† Everybody went out to have fun. I didn't have to do anything. But I had always lived in tough circumstances and never simply had fun. It wasn't in my nature. Until then I had never played around in my life.

I had learned how to do zazen at Eiheiji, so I went into the back room to practice. At that time one of the women who helped prepare the food for the festival entered the room to put the bowls she'd cleaned on the shelf in the back room. She was cleaning up after the ceremony. She opened the sliding doors where I was

---

* A festival when the spirits of the dead are believed to return home.

† *Segaki* is a ceremony where food is put out to feed the hungry ghosts.

practicing zazen. Normally I was accustomed to her bossing me around, but this time she repeated *namukiebutsu, namukiebutsu* [praise to the Buddha] with complete devotion. Here she was, this woman who would usually push me around, repeating this chant, being extremely reverent. How could she change into such a reverent woman? It was because of zazen. She didn't have any learning, but just automatically recited *namukiebutsu*. I hadn't studied anything about Buddhism at that time. Had I known more about Buddhism as I do now, it might have been different, but I didn't know anything. So I figured it must be [the power] of zazen. It felt miraculous—the real thing captured me first; study came later. Study alone is like [collecting] the dregs. Study should come after.

Then I went to Kyushu.

UEYAMA. After this?

SAWAKI. Yes, I went to Amakusa in Kyushu without a cent. I had a lot of hardships [on the trip].

UEYAMA. You walked?

SAWAKI. That's right.

UEYAMA. What prompted you to do that?

SAWAKI. What prompted me? Eiheiji was boring.* Staying there was meaningless. I was told that there was a place for me at Amakusa. My older Dharma brother said he would give me the money for the trip, but when I took him up on it, he said he didn't have any. I didn't want to go back to papering lanterns, so I decided to go anyway. It was a difficult trip. But I thought it would work out if only I could make it there.

* I assume Sawaki meant they were not serious about zazen.

UEYAMA. Horyuji. *Yuishiki* [Consciousness Only], wasn't it? Roshi studied *Yuishiki* Buddhism there, didn't you?

SAWAKI. Yes.

UEYAMA. Were you influenced in your later years by those studies?

SAWAKI. We studied *Yuishiki*. It was even studied in Kusharon.* It was the basis for [later] Buddhism.

UEYAMA. I see, and Zen goes beyond those studies.

SAWAKI. Yes, it goes beyond *Yuishiki*. *Yuishiki* was considered heresy [*both laugh*]. When I became a teacher at Komazawa University, they didn't know that I had a background in *Yuishiki*. They thought I'd been selling a product without the proper scale. Since I was teaching at the university, it was good that I had that background. It wasn't necessary for teaching Zen, but since it was a university it helped. I was once told that it was dangerous to practice Zen without a background in early Buddhism.†

So when the war was over—

UEYAMA. The Russo-Japanese War?

SAWAKI. Yes. So when the war was over, I went there [to Horyuji]. I was free to do whatever I wanted, so I went there for seven or eight years. I didn't have a place to go. Because I didn't have to go to my [adoptive parents'] home, I began to study the *Shobogenzo*. Then at Horyuji I studied other texts.

---

* A scripture that was brought to China from India and entered Japan in the Nara period.

† Sawaki is referring to the advice he received from Fueoka Roshi when he was a novice monk.

UEYAMA. However, [given] Zen's special character, I would think it would be difficult to teach.

SAWAKI. Well, Bodhidharma said, "*kakunen musho*" [being empty, there is no such thing as the holy truth]. Even the tiniest subjective thought is no good. Just follow the truth.

UEYAMA. I see. Follow the truth.

SAWAKI. Don't follow your own point of view. *Ken* is opinion or viewpoint.

UEYAMA. You cease following your own viewpoint?

SAWAKI. You hold to the truth.

UEYAMA. You hold to the truth?

SAWAKI. It's the way things are. Everyone sees things differently. That's a problem.

UEYAMA. Aha!

SAWAKI. Follow the truth. We each experience things differently. Viewpoints are different for all of us. Our battle with ideas is a result of differing viewpoints. In the end all we can do is keep quiet.

UEYAMA. [*laughs*]

SAWAKI. There's nothing we can do about it other than to just sit.

UEYAMA. If you say that ... [what about] today's science ...? That upon which modern civilization has developed? Rather than just being quiet, little by little we can develop reason that will be accepted and that people will study as [part of our] general culture. I feel it is completely different from what you are teaching about Zen.

SAWAKI. Yes, it is different.

UEYAMA. From the standpoint of Zen, does this feel wrong?

SAWAKI. There's no end to science.

UEYAMA. I see. And Zen is different.

SAWAKI. Science will swallow you up. Zen is about the truth. There is no beginning and no end. It's the same for the ancients and for modern man. It's the same world for all of humanity, isn't it?

UEYAMA. Yes.

SAWAKI. Science has developed [to this point] and still all humans of this world suffer. The push of one button . . . We can say it is crazy. If one disturbed person, [whoever it may be] pushes the button, it's the same catastrophe. Where is the modern, cultured man? It would be better if we all do zazen. Humans are absorbed in developing this scientific culture. They are eaten up by it. [*laughs*]

UEYAMA. You say that Zen is "things *as they are*." But there are many complicated things too, like the *Shobogenzo* and [studying] Buddhist *okesa*, which you, Roshi, are involved in.* And then there is the posture, which can be severe. Wouldn't it be better just to be?

SAWAKI. It's not really that difficult—things like zazen and *okesa*. What's important is how one feels. How you feel when you fold your *okesa* or when you practice zazen—like that cook's helper when she saw the zazen form when I was a child, and she bowed to it—that is the important thing. That's the meaning of

---

* *Okesa* is the Buddhist surplice, the robe worn by Buddhist priests. Sawaki researched the original robes and how they were sewed and started a movement sewing robes in the form of the original ones in Japan.

the saying "Manner is the Buddha Dharma." It is the form in which Dogen Zenji strongly believed, the importance of the form. That is the meaning of this form. When I put on this *okesa* and practice zazen, I don't need anything else.

UEYAMA. I see.

SAWAKI. So, when I put on this *okesa* and practice zazen, it is *anjin ryumei* [settling one's body and life].

Then I don't need anything. It doesn't matter whether or not I have book learning. I don't have to throw away what I have, nor do I have to attain anything I don't have.

They call my practice the *Okesa* sect.

UEYAMA. [*laughs*]

SAWAKI. I am referred to as the *Okesa* sect priest, because we put on *okesa* and practice zazen. That is the essence.

UEYAMA. In that case, what is the Zen position on the precepts—the five precepts and the ten precepts?

SAWAKI. The precepts are a result of someone doing something wrong. Every time someone transgresses, the Buddha would scold him. For example, if someone took someone else's property or took someone else's wife, each time something like that would happen [a precept was born]. Through Bodhidharma's *isshinkai* [single-minded precept], the ten precepts are transmitted. By transmitted it means awakened to, awakened to the Buddha mind, i.e., satori. Hence, understanding the Buddha's feeling is understanding the truth. That's why it is said that Zen and the precepts are the same. If you are practicing zazen you can't steal or take another's wife.

UEYAMA. That is Roshi's [behavior]. But we amateurs see the

origins as Shakamuni Buddha abandoning his home and becoming a home leaver. While monks today live in houses, they are not home leavers but rather home livers. They live lives very different from the monks of old [*laughs*]. What do you, Roshi, think about these modern monks?

SAWAKI. Well, it's become like a business [*chuckles*]. That's why Manzan [1635–1714] said, "To go from your parents' home to a substitute parent is no good." So they've been saying that from way back in the past. If you're not careful, it will become a business. But it should not be a business.

That's why I became a homeless monk. Kosho said, "You are a success."* [*laughs*] There are many ways to be successful. [*both laugh*] I couldn't ask for a better situation. There's nothing [I need to do], and I haven't felt any lack of freedom since I've come here.

UEYAMA. Well, most people would feel restricted [in your situation]. They would want to have a good position in life. And monks feel they want to increase the number of parishioners. Why do so many people gather under your guidance? To many it's a puzzle.

SAWAKI. Yes, well, I hated going on *takuhatsu* [begging].

UEYAMA. Ahh.

SAWAKI. There's this poem by Daichi Zenji:

We go to a poor village
Begging our food

---

* Kosho Uchiyama, Sawaki's main disciple and caretaker of Antaiji, where Sawaki spent his last years.

In the evening we return to the forest

And meditate

Following the way of the ancients.

In fact, this is something for which I am grateful.* I was busy traveling around Japan—leading monks on *takuhatsu* rounds. You have no spare time when doing *takuhatsu* . . . I was a master free-loader. [*both laugh*]

UEYAMA. Even Zen monks have families. Have you ever thought about having family around? For example, when we get old and become weak, we think about having family—having cute grandchildren around? You can think about it in comparison with your present life . . . Have you ever given thought to that kind of life?

SAWAKI. I don't have any children.

UEYAMA. Oh, really?

SAWAKI. Thank god! [*laughs*] With children and grandchildren, I would have to care for them. It wouldn't be easy. Now I don't have those restrictions. It's a good thing. I am grateful for that. I've been homeless and [now] I have this dilapidated place. It's fine. There are wild plants around here that are edible. People cook these wild vegetables for me, wild birds fly around here, the maples turn red in the fall; I am fortunate about everything.

UEYAMA. The last thing I want to ask you: What is Buddhism's place with regard to our modern society? What is its contribution? I think we are all interested in that.

---

* I assume "this" refers to following the way of the ancients.

SAWAKI. Buddhism's contribution? We really don't know Shakamuni Buddha. Why he left his home. What satori is. Shakamuni is supposed to have realized satori. What is that? That is the important matter. We really don't understand that. We really don't know. It's an extremely important matter. Not understanding this important matter, people build huge temples, which they leave us with. But what is the most important matter? If you think it is satori, you are making a big mistake. If you think it is religious practice, that too is a big mistake. It is to know the true Self, isn't it? We have to be in touch with what the true Self is.

From the time of our childhood we are all homeless. [*both laugh*] If you think you have a home, you are mistaken. Still people are fighting over homes.

UEYAMA. Do you mean that if everybody were homeless it would be a good thing? Wouldn't it create a very difficult situation?

SAWAKI. That they think they have homes is the problem.

UEYAMA. Where did Roshi come to that belief?

SAWAKI. [*laughs*] We never had a home from the beginning.

UEYAMA. Everyone begins without a home. That's why they build them.

SAWAKI. However you look at it, we are deluded. We make mistakes and these mistakes become customs. There's not much we can do about it.

UEYAMA. Thank you for taking the time to give this interview.

PART 3

Reflections

Kodo Sawaki holding hands with a child

At age thirty-three, Kodo Sawaki became *tanto* (monk in charge of training) at Yosenji Monastery in Matsuzaka City. Matsuzaka is located in Mie Prefecture, the same prefecture where Sawaki was born and raised. There he met Kozan Kato, who had just come down from a four-year solo retreat on Hazama Mountain. Kato was four years older than Sawaki. The two monks became instant friends.

In many respects they were an unlikely twosome. Kozan, originally a Soto priest, switched to Rinzai because, in his words, "there were no Soto temples where zazen was taken seriously." He spent five years at Shogenji in Ibuka, a severe Rinzai training monastery called the "devil's training monastery," before his solo retreat on Hazama Mountain. He was planning to go to Bairinji in Kurume, another "devil's training monastery," when he stopped at Yosenji. Sawaki's practice of *shikantaza* (just sitting) was in apparent contrast to Kato's koan Zen. Sawaki referred to koan Zen critically as "stepladder Zen," where one climbs the ladder seeking satori one rung at a time.

One thing that attracted them to each other in the short time they were together was a common sense of humor. What kept them together over the years was a strong belief in zazen, however different the mechanics for each man may have been.

Sawaki talked about how Kato left him behind when they both agreed that Yosenji was not the temple for them. Kato left the next morning on his way to Bairinji Monastery, leaving Sawaki to remark that he'd always been at the head of the pack, but Kato "left me in the dust." When they met again some years later, Kato told Sawaki he knew his friend had all those books and he didn't want to be commissioned to carry half of them. (Calling someone "bookish" is a way Zen students poke fun at each other.)

Another thing about Kato that earned Sawaki's respect was how diligently his friend followed the vow of poverty—a vow that was being ignored by many monks as Japan's economy grew before the Second World War.

After completing his Bairinji training with Komushitsu Roshi, Kato, in his characteristic manner, slipped away without informing anyone to a small temple in Okutama, a temple that had been uninhabited for twenty years. He'd been invited by a priest with whom he trained at Bairinji. The priest didn't tell him that the temple was dilapidated, or that most of the parishioners had abandoned it. It was more like a shack than a temple. Kato had a family and no means of making a living—begging was not a custom in that part of the country.

In 1936, Sawaki had been given a teaching post at Komazawa University and went to visit Kato at Tokuunin, his temple an hour's drive from Tokyo. When he saw the condition of the temple, he was shocked. He knew his friend followed the vow of poverty, and he respected Kato for that. But Kato had a wife and two children, so

Sawaki sought to help him. He contacted his patrons in Tokyo and asked them each to allow Kato to perform the monthly services at their altars. It was a common custom for monks to read sutras for the dead at the homes of parishioners. With a small vegetable garden and the money he received for the sutra readings, Kato and family were able to survive until the parishioners slowly came back to Tokuunin. The attraction of a monk with the status of Sawaki joining Kato every year for a New Year celebration was a primary reason for the parishioners returning. Kato's delightfully infectious personality was another.

. . .

Kozan Kato at ninety years old

Kozan Kato's Reflections on Kodo Sawaki

In 1969, Reverend Ryumin Akizuki, a Buddhist scholar and Zen priest, traveled to Okutama to interview Kozan Kato Roshi at his temple the Tokuunin. Roshi was ninety-three or ninety-four at the time. The story I heard from the late Kiyoshi Hoshi, professor of Buddhist philosophy and Zen student, was that Reverend Akizumi brought along a tape recorder that he concealed from Kato because Kato routinely asked people to forget about his talks as soon as they were over. That story was very possibly a myth created to elevate a man who needed no promotion.

. . .

No . . . Sawaki and I . . . friends?* . . . I was a poor monk and that fellow was a *zaibatsu*, so he took pity on me . . .† He was quite a colorful guy. He'd come here once a year on the second of January, without fail. He was given a post as professor at Komazawa University in Tokyo. From that year on for thirty years he'd show up on the second of January, never missing a day. What can I say about it? If I were an important person, I would understand it, but that wasn't the case. We talked about it once. "What kind of karma brought us together?" I asked. "Rotten

---

* Akizumi must have referred to Sawaki as his friend when he asked Kato about their relationship.

† *Zaibatsu*, a word used for a wealthy corporation—it was Kato's way of poking fun at his old buddy, who eschewed wealth as much as he did, though Sawaki was no longer alive to appreciate it.

karma" was his response. That's the way we talked. Finally, "We must have had some connection in a previous life," he said, and we both laughed.

During the war [World War II], there were constant air raids in Tokyo, and Kodo would come wearing a hard hat and a strange outfit resembling those worn by fishmongers—*mompei* work pants. He showed up on the second of January whether it rained or snowed or whatever else fell from the sky. You won't find people like that anymore. It was a wonderful connection.

Once he said to me, "Get yourself a pair of false teeth," and took out his purse. "I'll pay for it." [Kato had been toothless for over twenty years.] "I'll take the money," I said, "but I can do without the teeth." He shook his head and put away his purse.

When Kodo came to Tokuunin, the people around here were thrilled.* He would be in that room over there [*pointing to the room at the other end of the temple*], bullshitting and entertaining everybody. They enjoyed the New Year celebration because of his presence. That's the way it was when he was around. When he stopped coming for the New Year party, we all missed him.† People stopped coming. He was really special.

The last time he came here it was strange. He'd always come in good spirits. He would brush calligraphy and everyone would bring paper.‡ It was a custom to bring in the New Year—

---

* I assume by "people around here," he meant parishioners and friends of parishioners.

† In Sawaki's last two years, he could hardly walk and had to give up attending the Tokuunin New Year celebration.

‡ Scrolls, *shikishi*, etc.

something for them to take home as a souvenir. But that day Kodo got angry. "What do people expect from me? I'm not a street performer!"* He had a wild look on his face. When I returned to the room, I wondered what had happened. "Something feels wrong here," I said, and things settled down. I wondered what brought that anger on. It turned out that Kodo wanted me to brush the New Year calligraphy. When that fellow got angry, he didn't care who or what he screamed at, he just let it all out.

I had a lot of Kodo's calligraphy here; I even used some to patch up the ripped paper *fusuma* when it got old.† When the *fusuma* got too old and damaged, I would remove the calligraphy papers and place them under the veranda. When Kodo died, many people came, took them, and brought them to their homes and framed them. When it rained, one of the monks here found one in the garden, picked it up, and we framed it.

That day of the commotion Sawaki told me he wouldn't be coming the next year. I was eighty-eight at the time. "I'll come again for your ninetieth," he said.

That year, while giving a lecture—what month was it? He fell over and after that his legs could no longer carry him. It was as if he'd had a premonition; strange, wasn't it? His situation got bad and his disciple Kosho Uchiyama took him to Antaiji in Kyoto. I planned to visit him in Kyoto. This fellow Matsumoto said he

---

* The story as told by Kozan's disciple Yanase was a little different, and Kodo's anger was perhaps understandable, but Kozan was out of the room at the time. For Yanase's version, see Akizuki Ryomin and Yanase Yuzen, *Kobutsu Kozan* 古仏耕山 [Kozan the Old Buddha] (Tokyo: Hakujusha, 1983).

† Doors that are dividers from room to room that are made mostly of paper.

was going to Kyoto on business and that he would tell Kodo of my wish.* Sawaki's response was "That old fellow shuffling all the way here. What for? Tell him not to come." "That's fine," I said. That was the end of it. The following year he died, and I heard that he really wanted to see me.

But me and Kodo were like a paper lantern and a temple bell. He was a well-recognized scholar and I am illiterate. Still, we had a very special connection. That's fate for you! Even now, something happens and the thought of how special that fellow was rises up in me.

. . .

In 1934, Sodo Yokoyama started practicing zazen in a mountain near his home.† When a pheasant perched nearby and glared at him, he felt that zazen had some power that had nothing to do with his feelings as a human.

Three years later, Yokoyama's father died. The following month he attended a summer retreat and heard talks by Kodo Sawaki. He knew right away that he wanted to be a monk and to study under Sawaki. In Yokoyama's words:

Ah! This man's teaching [i.e., zazen] is the only [true] one in all of Japan. I felt it immediately. The average teacher's Dharma,

---

* A parishioner of Tokuunin.
† The following information comes from Yokoyama's diary entries in *The Wood Where I Stand*.

that is, someone other than Sawaki Roshi, could be followed by anyone. However, when it comes to Roshi's teaching, only someone like me, who as a child listened to my father talking and who played near him for long periods of time, was prepared for Roshi's Dharma.* In other words, there weren't many in this world raised as I was, so Roshi had to travel the country in order to find people willing to spend long hours practicing zazen. No matter how much people called him "Roshi, Roshi," in the end few of them took responsibility for actually practicing. When I intuited this, I decided to be ordained.

Sodo Yokoyama, the Grass Flute Zen Master
and disciple of Kodo Sawaki

* Yokoyama wrote about how at seven years old he saw his father practicing zazen. When his father said he was practicing like the Buddha, he took it as if the Buddha was practicing like his father.

. . .

Yokoyama's reflections on his teacher seem to be confined to Sawaki's Dharma. For Yokoyama, Sawaki *was* his teaching; hence the comments below are primarily of Sawaki's teaching on Buddhism and very little about the roshi's personality.

From Fukan zaso mihotoke 普勧坐相みほとけ *(The Universal Posture of the Buddha), edited by Joko Shibata*

"That which I call 'me' is completely a result of karma; zazen goes beyond karma."

Chou in nen hou means "the Way beyond karma"—superior, inferior; like and hate; philosophy, art, and science; these do not register with zazen. It's only natural that things created by humans, things that are a result of karma, in the face of the "Way beyond karma," are of no use. Therefore, zazen is of use for zazen alone.

Roshi [Sawaki] wants everyone to practice zazen, not to become superior and not because they will like it. What he wants is for people to practice the "Way beyond karma." He expressed his desire for people to know the meaning of "zazen is Buddhahood," or "zazen is Buddha Dharma," or "zazen is Buddha." That is all there is.

Words our teacher expressed to us until we had calluses on our ears were "Become yourself completely and you are Buddha." When you become yourself completely, then the "you" disappears. Nature is egoless, and that is Buddha.

The natural universe does not think like man does. Mountains are mountains, rivers are rivers, and the myriad things are naturally the Buddha, who is the Self being the Self completely. We call this the original Buddha ...

The Buddha Way is reality, so if you understand reality, knowing the Buddha Way is not difficult.

The spontaneous Buddha is the real thing. The real thing is Buddhahood unplanned.

[Sawaki] Roshi says *shikantaza* [just sitting] is the reality of the spontaneous Buddha—the reality of the non-planning Buddha. So persisting in zazen to the very end is the meaning of the real thing. *Shikantaza* is practicing zazen without any thought of what you will become. If you practice zazen, *that is it*—there is nothing more and nothing less; everything becomes zazen and that is its meaning.

Roshi's "zazen is zazen" is the principle of the universe—it is the meaning of suchness. So the myriad things are one. If we think of it in the now, the dandelion is a dandelion, the mountain is a mountain, and the river is a river, and I am I. I take refuge in myself, and I am never weary of myself; I am myself completely and take refuge in nothing outside of myself.

That's the way things are. The myriad things of the universe are all *as they are* when you give yourself up to them completely. That's why Roshi says, "Giving your all is Buddhahood," what he calls "the Way of the universe." That's why I do not hesitate in practicing a zazen which is "zazen equals zazen" [only].

We think of our lives as being lived solely on this earth. We think of ourselves as earth people. Though we regard dandelions as earth plants only, in fact this globe is a fine example of the heavens, and all phenomena on it are of the heavens. If the universe is the foundation for the earth and the stars, then it should include mankind. That's why Roshi says, "Everything is a continuation of the universe."

. . .

The following is taken from **The Grass Flute Zen Master**

It would be great if people came to listen to Roshi's talks because they wanted to practice zazen, but according to Roshi they come because of him. And he adds, "There is nothing I can do about it." It is nothing more than the result of karma. "Zazen," he said, "is the way beyond karma." It has nothing to do with likes, success, philosophy, the arts, etc. All of that is human creation, a result of karma. So it's natural that zazen, in the light of that, has no particular benefit. Zazen is useful for zazen only. Roshi wants everyone to practice this kind of zazen, and not to practice because they think he is special. He truly follows the Way beyond cause and effect. He wants people to understand the meaning: "Zazen equals Buddhahood," "Zazen equals Buddha Dharma."

"To practice is to die." These words of Roshi's mean that zazen is the death of the ego, so one is in harmony with the universe. To live eternally with the universe is the way of the parents [ancestors].

. . .

From a letter by Yokoyama to Masanori Yuna, founder of the Tokyo Kendo Association, written on February 28, 1977. Translated in Living and Dying in Zazen.*

My teacher, the late Sawaki Roshi, often made the following self-evaluation: "I am an extremely deluded person. Nobody is as deluded as I am. I am deluded with gold trimmings."

What a strange thing this zazen is. When we practice it, distracting ideas, irrelevant thoughts—in short, delusions, which ordinary people are made of—suddenly seem to feel an irresistible temptation to arise and appear at the surface. Then there is a desire to drive those thoughts away, an irresistible desire to which our complete effort is added. Those who don't meditate know nothing about this. Why is it that when we practice, deluded thoughts continue to surface, one after the other? The reason, which we learn from zazen, is that each one of us, from prince to beggar, is an ordinary [deluded] person. The attempt to drive those deluded thoughts away—delusion being so much nonsense [interfering with the happiness of oneself and others]—is also something brought home to us through zazen. We tentatively call this zazen that guides us in this way "Buddha."

According to this teaching, simply the awareness that you are deluded, which comes from practicing zazen, makes you, in real-

* See *Living and Dying in Zazen*, 44–48, for Yokoyama's full letter to Masanori Yuno, the founder of the Tokyo Kendo Association.

ity, a Buddha. It's zazen that teaches us that we too are deluded, and hence delivers us from this delusion. When we actually practice zazen and look carefully at all the deluded ideas that keep popping up, we realize how ordinary we are, and how little we have to be proud of or to brag about—nothing to do other than quietly hide away. This is, after all, what we truly are.

Satori is being enlightened to the fact that we are deluded.

. . .

Kosho Uchiyama, the late abbot of Antaiji Temple
and disciple of Kodo Sawaki

Kosho Uchiyama was ordained by Kodo Sawaki in 1941. He studied with Sawaki until the roshi's death in 1965, and then became abbot of Antaiji, a temple he'd been caretaker of while Sawaki traveled the country until the roshi's legs failed him in the last two years of his life. Uchiyama cared for his teacher together with a nun named Joshin Kasai and another nun named Kobun Okamoto. Others came to help at Antaiji when Roshi needed full-time care.

. . .

From "Recollections of My Teacher, Kodo Sawaki Roshi"

My translation is taken from the Japanese in the last chapter of Yadonashi Hokusan 宿なし法句参 (The Dharma of Homeless Kodo).*

Kodo Sawaki Roshi is commonly acknowledged as the driving force behind restoring the practice of *shikantaza*, or "just sitting," within Soto Zen, the tradition founded by Dogen Zenji. The goal of this practice is not some special enlightenment separate from sitting. Because of this "nothing special" attitude, even people in the Soto school didn't take zazen seriously for a long time before Sawaki Roshi appeared . . .

Because people who wanted to practice usually went to Rinzai temples and studied koans, it must have been difficult initially to encourage people to just sit. However, because of his charisma,

---

* For a complete translation of this essay, see Uchiyama and Okumura, *The Zen Teaching of Homeless Kodo*, 231–34.

unique karmic attributes, and the power of his own diligent practice, Sawaki Roshi successfully achieved this mission . . .

Wherever [Sawaki] went, people were attracted to him like iron to a magnet. Sometimes the power of his personality could be overpowering. For instance, when he said "Zazen is good for nothing," people were caught by his personality and thought, "Even though Roshi says this in words, zazen must bring us some benefit." Although he convinced people to sit, they didn't always understand why.

Sawaki Roshi practiced more conscientiously than anyone. I became his disciple at Daichuji Temple in Tochigi Prefecture on December 8, 1941. At the time he was in his sixties, and during *sesshin* at Daichuji the wake-up bell rang at 2:50 a.m. But Roshi started to sit at 1:30. We sat until 10:00 p.m. He slept only a few hours at night. He practiced this way for five days a month as well as a week during Rohatsu, the celebration of the Buddha's enlightenment.

When he saw practitioners slack off, even a little, he scolded and goaded us with his thunderous voice as if a huge temple bell were shaking. Drawn by his power, practitioners were able to just sit the zazen that has nothing to do with satori . . .

Relatively speaking, Sawaki Roshi was a good-natured old man [when he settled] at Antaiji. By relaxing his authority, he taught us that zazen is "the most honored one" and we could practice more spontaneously, from our own motivation rather than from external pressure . . .

Viewing zazen as the most honored one determined our attitude toward our whole lives. What should our outlook be?

Here's my best attempt to express what my teacher inscribed in my mind.

- Gaining is delusion and losing is realization.
- Don't try to get any benefit. Don't be greedy, and don't regret losing.
- Never establish an organization. Things achieved by an institution will collapse because of that institution. The rise and fall of accomplishments is nothing other than the transmigration within samsara. This was Sawaki Roshi's fundamental attitude.
- Teach individuals one by one. Rather than educating people generally within a system, we need to address each individually, since each is unique.
- Don't ask for donations. People have the idea that if they're involved in a temple, they'll be asked to donate. This has seriously injured the Buddha Dharma. We never ask for donations. That way people can come without worrying about money.
- Don't be fickle. Don't act pulled by your self-centered thoughts.
- If you're careless, you'll become famous and achieve a high position. Make every effort not to rise in the world. Particularly after age forty, fame and profit will be tempting.

Each of these instructions at first glance may sound straightforward. Yet when you look closely, you'll find that they are not the mainstream teaching of this world. Sawaki Roshi not only taught these sayings, he practiced them as an example . . .

Whenever I encounter trouble, [these teachings] come to mind, and I find my teacher is still instructing me. I am deeply grateful for this.

Gudo Nishijima, one-time student of Kodo Sawaki

Gudo Wafu Nishijima

Gudo Nishijima was born in Yokohama, Japan in November 1919. He graduated from the Law Department of Tokyo University in September 1946. In October 1940, he first attended a retreat by Kodo Sawaki, and he continued to study with him until Sawaki's death in 1965. During that time, while working at the Japanese Ministry of Finance, he practiced zazen daily and studied Dogen's *Shobogenzo*.

In 1973, Nishijima was ordained by Rempo Niwa, and he received Dharma transmission from Niwa Roshi in December 1977. Niwa subsequently became abbot of Eiheiji Monastery.

During the 1960s, Nishijima, one of the few English-speaking Zen masters, began offering regular lectures in Buddhism and Zen meditation. He attracted a number of Western disciples, including Mike Luetchford—who was an heir to Nishijima's Dharma teachings and the founder of Dogen Sangha UK—and Jeffrey Bailey, who together with Nishijima co-authored *To Meet the Real Dragon*. Also among these early disciples were Zen Dharma teacher Jundo Cohen and author Brad Warner. Working with his disciple Mike Chodo Cross, Nishijima translated Dogen's *Shobogenzo*.*

. . .

The following is an excerpt taken from a blog by Gudo Nishijima called "Dogen Sangha Blog."†

I have had two reverend masters who taught me directly. One is Master Kodo Sawaki, and the other is Master Rempo Niwa.

* Gudo Nishijima and Chodo Cross, trans., *Master Dogen's Shobogenzo*, 4 vols. (Tokyo: Windbell Publications, 1994–99).
† Excerpt of Gudo Nishijima, "Dogen Sangha (4) The Two Reverend Masters" *Dogen Sangha Blog*, August 15, 2006, gudoblog-e.blogspot.com/2006/08/dogen -sangha-4-two-reverend-masters.html. Edited for errors and inconsistencies.

In October of 1940, I was fortunate to learn that Master Kodo Sawaki would have a *Sesshin* at Daichuji, a temple in Tochigi Prefecture. I attended it carrying rice in a clothes bag, because it was a time when the Japanese food situation had become very bad.

In the morning we got up at three o'clock, and we practiced zazen for two sittings, forty-five minutes each, two times before breakfast, two times in the morning after breakfast, two times in the afternoon, and once at night. Master Kodo Sawaki presented his Buddhist lectures two times a day, one in the morning and one in the afternoon. While listening to his Buddhist lecture, I realized that I was hearing a true Buddhist lecture for the first time. His voice was very loud and strong, and his message was so understandable and so persuasive.

The textbook he used for the lecture was the *Fukan-Zazen-Gi*. *Fukan-Zazen-Gi* was the first book that Master Dogen wrote after coming back from China, and, in fact, the first book he wrote in his life. Master Kodo Sawaki had studied the Buddhist philosophy called the Hosso School, which was established in Tang Dynasty China. Kodo studied it in his younger years, and so his Buddhist philosophy was very complete. When he was young he studied Hosso Sect theory under Join Saeki in Horyuji temple, and so even though his Buddhism was established through his practice of zazen, at the same time his philosophical structure was also very logical and exact.

At the same time, I think that the most excellent point of Master Kodo Sawaki's Buddhism was his absolute pure attitude as he pursued the truth. In *Shobogenzo* there is a chapter called "Ju-Undo-Shiki." And in it Master Dogen says, "A person who has the will to seek the Truth, and who has the intention to throw away fame and profit, can enter [the Way]. A person who does not sincerely seek the Truth should not be allowed to enter. If there are some who are not sincere and have been admitted by mistake, we should, after consideration, make them leave.* We should notice that if we have the will to follow the Truth, we will become free from fame and profit."

Master Kodo Sawaki clearly knew this fundamental Buddhist principle in his practiced Buddhist life. Therefore he didn't want to own a temple throughout his life. He realized that if a Buddhist monk has his own temple, his job to manage the temple would leave him so busy it would be impossible for him to study the true Buddhist teachings thoroughly. Therefore Master Kodo Sawaki never married, and he devoted his whole life to promote Buddhism.

* I have changed this last sentence to be in accord with Dogen's words as translated by Nishijima in his English-language *Shobogenzo*. See *Shobogenzo*, Book 1, 45, "Ju-Undo-Shiki: Rules for the Hall of Heavy Cloud."

Kodo Sawaki and Kosho Uchiyama walking in the garden at Antaiji
Temple *(Photograph courtesy of Daihorin Publishers)*

Kodo Sawaki was born in a chaotic environment and spent the first
quarter of a century fighting his way out of that chaos. His desire to
escape from the world of corruption and enter what he perceived

in his youth as a world of beauty was to inform most of his life from the time he ran away from his adoptive parents and from Ishinden in his seventeenth year.

Sawaki, or Saikichi, his given name, was a tough street urchin, and that toughness didn't simply disappear because he decided in his mind that he no longer wanted to be tough. The contradiction between his lingering street behavior and his imagined world of beauty followed him until his dying days.

. . .

When I moved into Antaiji Temple in the summer of 1969, a tall young American who was leaving Japan after training at Antaiji for at least a half year said to me, "Uchiyama Roshi's teacher [Sawaki] was considered the foremost scholar of Dogen Zenji in Japan." I don't know where he got that information, but I assume it was from some of the Antaiji monks. I don't think of Sawaki as a Dogen scholar, but I would agree with Kosho Uchiyama that Kodo Sawaki is "commonly acknowledged as the driving force behind restoring the practice of shikantaza, or just sitting [zazen], within Soto Zen."

Whether or not Sawaki was a foremost Dogen scholar, he was certainly schooled in the Buddhist teachings within Soto Zen as well as the teachings of other Buddhist sects. I see him more as a popularizer of Zen practice, in the best sense of the word. His love of zazen was infectious, inspiring more people to the practice than any other teacher or scholar of Zen in twentieth-century Japan could honestly claim.

. . .

As Sawaki told Shunke Ueyama, who came to interview him at Antaiji in Sawaki's final year, "I hadn't studied anything about Buddhism when I first arrived at Eiheiji in my seventeenth year." When one of the women who helped cook and clean for a ceremony at a sister temple of Eiheiji walked in on Sawaki when he was practicing zazen and bowed reverently to him, he was convinced that it was zazen and not him that she was bowing to. It was the power of zazen that could penetrate the mind of a seventeen-year-old novice who'd yet to read anything about Buddhism and of a temple helper who was a simple, uneducated woman. From that day on, he vowed to practice zazen and believed it important to understand before endeavoring to study the scriptures.

Sawaki also explained to Ueyama why he went into the back room when all the other monks took advantage of the free day to go to town and have fun.

"I'd always lived in tough circumstances and never simply had fun. It wasn't in my nature. Until then, I'd never played around in my life."

To a young man who had to care for his abusive adoptive parents, work in their lantern-making shop in their stead, look out for the police who would occasionally raid his family's gambling casino, and deal with unsavory people on a daily basis, sitting quietly in zazen may have felt like a relief after having lived that hectic life in Ishinden. The relief lasted long enough for him to eventually understand the truth of "a zazen that gives you nothing." Once he spent time in zazen—slowing down long enough to look inside and experience his true Self—the practice became his life. There were trying times, but he never lost faith in zazen. His old habits recurred at times, but they never turned him around. They only made him realize that he was flawed too like all sentient beings, and that practicing within the turmoil was true practice.

Sawaki's understanding from the Pure Land Buddhism of his childhood that we are all deluded people who are saved by the vow of Amida Buddha added a depth to his understanding of Zen, which allowed him to appeal to monastics and laypeople alike.

· · ·

This book is subtitled "Kodo Sawaki's Art of Zen Meditation." It is considered an art, and like most art it is derived from a subjective experience. Sawaki's statement "I practice a zazen that comes to nothing" can be off-putting to many who come to meditation practice with the hope of improving themselves. This statement, however, is a stroke of genius. It is not Sawaki's creation—it goes back to the Heart Sutra and beyond—but his insistence on repeating it—driving it home, so to speak—is Sawaki's "art." Practicing a zazen that comes to nothing can be thought of as leaving your ego at the entrance to the meditation hall.

It was suggested that I use a different (more acceptable) translation for Sawaki's zazen wa nanimo narimasen (zazen comes to nothing), something like "a zazen that has no attainment." I prefer "comes to nothing," because it better expresses the personality of the man who stated it—a statement by a man who for most of his life was an outsider.

· · ·

Having come of age in a community of disreputable people, truthfulness—something he rarely came across in Ishinden—became Sawaki's code of behavior, which he adopted for his whole life.

He hadn't run off to Eiheiji because of the teaching of its founder; in fact, he knew nothing of the teaching of Dogen. He picked Eiheiji because it was far enough away from Ishinden that his adoptive parents wouldn't be able to find him and bring him back home.

When he did study Dogen, the ancient master's insistence on living in poverty, stress on the unity of practice and enlightenment in zazen, and attention to detail resonated so much with his own understanding that it felt like Dogen was speaking directly to him.

While he was very caring to his disciples, his insistence on the principles Dogen taught, and on the long hours of zazen, surprisingly made him a kind of outsider to the general Zen community. This was compounded by his habit of denigrating monks who took advantage of their positions in the hierarchy of the Zen community to live comfortably and treat their temples as—what he called—Zen businesses.

Sawaki never charged money for his talks or retreats (though he was given donations) and he printed pamphlets of the texts he used for his talks with his own money and gave them to his audience free of charge. He also sponsored students who wanted to study at Komazawa University but who didn't have money for tuition.

Setting an example as a monk living in poverty at a time when Japan was slowly becoming an affluent nation did not endear Sawaki to much of the twentieth-century Zen world. But to a small group of devotees who respected his authenticity and his attempt to live like the Zen monks of antiquity, it earned him great respect.

. . .

I would like to end with some excerpts from the Kodo Sawaki chapter in *Living and Dying in Zazen*, a book I wrote in 2003:

I once received an audiotape of one of Sawaki's final lectures, delivered when he moved to Antaiji at the end of his life.

"Kodo Sawaki Roshi lectures on Dogen Zenji's *Bendowa*. This tape was recorded in the spring of 1964 at Antaiji Temple in Kyoto." The recorded voice speaks over the somber tones of chanting.

Then a strong, gruff voice takes over—it is Kodo Sawaki in his eighty-third year.

"The *Bendowa* is the first chapter of the *Shobogenzo*."

Sawaki explains the origin of the text, where the first copy was discovered, and who found it. He talks about the meaning of the characters that make up the title *Bendowa*. The character *ben* means power or energy and *do* stands for way. So it means put energy into the Way. The expression "Bendowa" came from the Record of Wanshi Zenji.

After quoting Wanshi's use of the word, Sawaki equates *bendo* with zazen. He proceeds to read from the text. "All Buddhas together have been simply transmitting this wondrous Dharma . . . The wondrous Dharma, which has been transmitted only from Buddha to Buddha without deviation, has as its criterion *jijuyu samadhi*."

"*Jijuyu samadhi*," Sawaki explains, "is 'zazen that comes to noth-

ing.' You have to forget any results of your effort. Result-oriented practice is merely an enterprise, a business. Monks say that they have no
time to do zazen."

"I always say zazen is an activity that comes to nothing," he re-
peats. "There is nothing more admirable than this activity that comes
to nothing."

"To do something with a goal is really worthless." The inevitable
Zen paradox.

These opening words give a wonderful summary of the teaching
of this unique Zen personality. Though Sawaki's health was failing
when he gave this lecture, his voice is clear and vibrant.

I imagine him unable to use his legs any longer and being carried down from his second-floor room at Antaiji by a few disciples.
He gets behind the table, opens his text, and an explosive energy
emerges from him: a *bendowa*, a putting of energy into the Way. He
is a scholar—talking of the origins of the *Bendowa*, the influence on
Dogen when he wrote it, and Dogen's unusual use of the Japanese
and Chinese languages. He is a rebel—badmouthing the Zen institu-
tions with their lazy clerics. But most of all, he is waving a banner for
zazen—the zazen known as *shikantaza*, or just sitting, a zazen that he
insists has absolutely no value in the sense of progress, benefit, or, in
his everyday language, "paybacks." "Because it takes you out of the
world of loss and gain," he says, "it should be practiced."

. . .

When Sawaki first came to settle at Antaiji in June 1963, he was
walking in the garden, but by the spring of 1965 he could only

leave his second-floor room once every ten days. He spent his last days reading in his room.

As early as the fall of 1963, he was already talking about his end. Tadao Tanaka, his biographer, visited him and quoted him as saying, "I know death must be coming soon, though I don't feel its presence one bit." Long before he was forced to settle at Antaiji, he had his last will and testament hanging on his person. It stated, "If this rustic monk is found dead by the roadside, take his body to a nearby university to be dissected and used for research." He always carried five thousand yen, which he requested be used to transport his corpse, with a tip for the trouble he'd caused.

. . .

Tanaka quoted Sawaki as saying in 1965, "It's difficult for me to go up and down the stairs, so they have to carry the washbasin up to me here. Uchiyama, Joshin, and others bathe me. I'm like a newborn baby." Sawaki would try to make them laugh while they bathed him. When they finished and he was relaxing, feeling better, he would say, "I'm so lucky" and "This is too good for me."

Tanaka writes, "There were ten of us in the room one day that summer, and Roshi talked for twenty minutes about the lines 'How many miles from the floating world / Mountain cherry' from a well-known Japanese poem. But his voice was not as in the old days, and it was not unusual to see his whole body or his hands shaking. I thought of the great monks of old, and I felt his deterioration and was filled with emotion. Tears started to roll down my face and I went to the toilet and cried my eyes out."

. . .

From Sawaki's window you could see Takagamine, one of the three peaks in the northwest of Kyoto. This was the peak where Tosui, an Edo period Zen eccentric, spent his final days. Tosui, like Jittoku, Kanzan, and Hotei, was a character Sawaki often referred to with great respect. One of the final joys of Sawaki's life was looking out at Takagamine and watching the clouds pass over the peak. Tosui composed a poem in which he spent his final days gazing at Takagamine Peak. I'm sure Sawaki's joy at looking out at the peak was partly from knowing that one of his favorite eccentrics shared the same pleasure more than two hundred years earlier.

. . .

With Sawaki's failing health and continued confinement to bed, he turned his attention more and more to Takagamine Mountain. He could gaze out at it through the southern window while lying there. It was lying there beside him. He had spent much of his life in the mountains throughout Japan, living in them and walking through them, and watching his beloved Takagamine proved to be an important consolation in his final days.

Sawaki had been in a coma for some days when he stopped breathing at 1:50 a.m. on December 21. In accord with his wishes, he was taken to the autopsy room at the Kyoto University Medical School. Word of his death spread and many friends and disciples who lived nearby came to the dissection room to get a last look at Roshi's face.

ACKNOWLEDGMENTS

Zen chishiki 善知識 translates as "a good friend"—an epithet for one's teacher in Zen—and is the best way I can describe the people who helped with this book.

Thanks to Don Sweetbaum and Vincent Mowrey, excellent readers and writers and truly good friends.

Thanks to Reverend Shohaku Okumura, who has always been available to answer my questions about Kodo Sawaki, his teacher's teacher.

Thanks to Reverend Shusoku Kushiya, who let me translate from the books he edited of Kodo Sawaki's talks, and put me in contact with Hirotoshi Koyama of Daihorin Publishers. And thanks to Mr. Koyama for sending me photos that I used for the book.

Thanks once more to Hiroko, my partner, for answering my countless questions regarding Sawaki's unique and colloquial expressions.

And, of course, thanks to Jack Shoemaker and the Counterpoint team, who know how to make a writer feel good about his work.

© Hiroko Braverman

ARTHUR BRAVERMAN is an author, translator, and student of Zen Buddhism. He grew up in New York City and became interested in Zen Buddhism in his early twenties. After serving two years in the U.S. Peace Corps in Nigeria, he went to Japan to practice meditation. There he met Kosho Uchiyama and decided to practice at Antaiji in Kyoto studying the writing of Dogen. His previous translations include *Mud and Water: The Teachings of Zen Master Bassui*, *Warrior of Zen: The Diamond-hard Wisdom Mind of Suzuki Shoson*, and *A Quiet Room: The Poetry of Zen Master Jakushitsu*. He lives in Ojai, California, with his wife.